Captivated

Your One Wild
and Precious Life
and the Loving
Outrageousness of Jesus

TOM A. JONES

Captivated: Your One Wild and Precious Life and the Loving Outrageousness of Jesus

ISBN: 978-1-958723-39-5. Copyright © 2024 by Tom A. Jones.

All rights reserved. No part of this publication may be reproduced, stored in a retrieval system, or transmitted in any form or by any means—electronic, mechanical, digital, photocopy, recording, or any other—except for brief quotations in printed reviews, without the permission of the author and publisher.

Theatron Press titles may be purchased in bulk for classroom instruction, business, fund-raising, or sales promotional use. For information, please e-mail us at info@ipibooks.com. We care deeply about using renewable resources and uses recycled paper whenever possible.

All Scripture quotations, unless otherwise indicated, are from *The Holy Bible, New International Version,* Copyright © 1973, 1978, 1984, 2011 by Biblica, Inc. Used by permission. All rights reserved worldwide.

Interior layout: Toney Mulhollan. Cover design by Roy Appalsamy.

About the author: Tom A. Jones makes his home in the New Orleans area. Tom is the author of *No One Like Him: Jesus and His Message, The Baptized Life, Deep Convictions, God's Perfect Plan for Imperfect People, In Search of a City,* and many other books.

Theatron Press is an imprint of Illumination Publishers International.

www.ipibooks.com

CONTENTS

	Introduction	5
1.	Your	11
2.	One	17
3.	Wild	21
4.	Precious	31
5.	Life	35
6.	Outrageous	47
7.	Insanely Generous	57
8.	Abba? How Dare You?	69
9.	Even My Enemies?	87
10.	Jesus, Yes. Church, No.	99
11.	No Way!	109
12.	The Life? Yes, the Life.	115
13.	Captivated	129
	Postscript to Those Who Once "Decided"	137
	Cast of Characters	143
	More About Jesus and "Church"	146
	End Notes	151

To
Sheila Presley Jones
1948-2022

You greatly blessed the life
of your husband and
three precious daughters.
And many others.

Introduction

If you have read any of my previous books, after you read a while in this one, you may be asking, is this really by the same guy? Where in the world did this come from? Is this what happens when people get older? Did he run this idea by anyone? What genre would you put this one in?

I have wondered if some may find this little volume a bit... well, quirky. Just for fun I asked Merriam-Webster for some synonyms for quirky. There were many, including: eccentric, odd, strange, peculiar, weird, bizarre, and wild. I hope this book will not deserve most of those labels, but as you will see, I won't mind "wild."[1] Just so you know, I'm not going for quirky but I am going for wild. But I will say more about that word shortly.

One of the things that makes this book different from anything else I've written is this: This book was inspired by a poem, And I am a person who's never been drawn to poetry. My late wife, Sheila, with whom I spent almost 53 years, wrote poetry and loved to read poetry. While we were dating, we almost broke up over the issue of poetry. I still remember exactly where we had that conversation. (But we eventually united on things more important.) I think there's something about my brain that just doesn't "get it" when it comes to poetry, and that is a weakness of mine I wish I could fix. But, then again, I might be making progress. Here I am, these many years later, starting a book off talking about a poem that has majorly affected me and a poet I will quote quite often.

Mary Oliver was one of America's best-loved poets of the twentieth and twenty-first centuries. She died in 2019 at age eighty-three. I was introduced to Mary Oliver by one of my daughters, and this old prose guy found himself connecting with her poetry. Mary once wrote that there are three rules for life: 1) Pay attention, 2) Be in awe, and 3) Tell someone. And by the way, those eight words have changed the life of this 77-year-old writer, especially as they have intersected with spiritual truths that I will share in part two of this book. And all that happened after I turned 75. There is hope for us old guys.

On one day, probably in the 1980s, Mary was paying attention. She wrote the poem titled "The Summer

Day." It was first published in 1990. I have made arrangements with her estate to reprint it. Here are her words and you might want to read them aloud:

"The Summer Day"

Who made the world?
Who made the swan, and the black bear?
Who made the grasshopper?
This grasshopper, I mean–
the one who has flung herself out of the grass,
the one who is eating sugar out of my hand,
who is moving her jaws back and forth instead of up and down–
who is gazing around with her enormous and complicated eyes.
Now she lifts her pale forearms and thoroughly washes her face.
Now she snaps her wings open, and floats away.
I don't know exactly what a prayer is.
I do know how to pay attention, how to fall down
into the grass, how to kneel down in the grass,
how to be idle and blessed, how to stroll through the fields,
which is what I have been doing all day.
Tell me, what else should I have done?
Doesn't everything die at last, and too soon?

> Tell me, what is it you plan to do
> with your one wild and precious life?

Mary Oliver often wrote her poetry after, or even during, her nature walks. But her walks in the outdoors often led her to reflect on our inner lives. Her gentle words here pack a powerful punch. "Your one wild and precious life." You and I, we get one life—only one—and it's wild and it's precious. What is our plan?

In the chapters to come, in part one of this book, we're going to take those words one by one: *Your. One. Wild. Precious. Life.* Then in part two we'll look at how those words intersect with the loving outrageousness of Jesus. I have tried to pay attention. I have been left in awe, and now I have to tell someone. So, you have been chosen, and I invite you along for the ride. We all know it will be imperfect, but let's see if it will be quirky, strange, bizarro, or wild. Let's see if it might land somewhere in the midst of our ache and our longing and our need.

Part 1

Chapter 1

Your

The word *your* applies to you in many ways. Let's start with your book that you are holding right now (or your electronic reader). It's yours. Then there are your car keys that you will need if you want to drive your car that is outside in your driveway or in your designated parking spot. On the way out, don't forget to pick up your phone. Probably no one else in the world has all the exact same numbers saved as you do. As you drive, you may turn on your favorite radio station. Maybe it is a sports station and you want to hear about your favorite team. Or not. Maybe your favorite music is smooth jazz. When you get back to your apartment tonight, it will be time to eat your dinner. And then you'll head for the bathroom to get your toothbrush, not someone else's (yuck), and then you will go to your bedroom where you'll find your special pillow. Ahh!

A lot of things belong to us, and much is associated with us, probably much more than we realize. Some of you have your girlfriend or your boyfriend, your husband or your wife. Some of you have your children and the responsibility for them. I can say that all of you have your birthday and it is probably unique in your family. Unless you are a twin or one of triplets.

But then, let me go on to your pride and joy: your dog or your cat, and here we have something that's yours that has both an upside and a downside, but mostly an upside. You love your furry friend, but then there's your responsibility to make sure he or she is fed and goes out to do their business. And then, oh yes, there is your bill from the vet that your pet has no plans to help out with. But, still, you love them.

Now if you are an American or a Canadian, or a citizen of many of the free countries in the world, you may be noticing that I've left out some very important things. Those would be your rights. If there is anything Americans prize, it is their rights. Soon after the American Constitution was written, the Bill of Rights was quickly added: ten amendments spelling out the rights of every American. As a citizen, these are your rights, and you probably value them. But there is something else that is yours. It's not spelled out in the Constitution, but you also have your responsibility. With your rights come your responsibilities. It is a problem to have the former without the latter.

Your. It is a small word that we likely use dozens of times every day, but when you stop and meditate on it, you start realizing there are a lot of things, both good and bad, that are yours.

Let's not forget, of course, your looks. Some of us don't really care about all them, but some of us some of us care a lot. And it seems that many people are not happy about their looks. I don't know the latest, but for a long time South Korea led the world in plastic surgeries per capita. It is integrated into daily life. There are dozens of advertisements for it in subway stations, buses, and streets. Parents often "gift" their children some form of surgery after they finish their national college entrance exams or when they become legal adults. South Korean TV programs showcase the wonders of plastic surgery and how it can transform entire lives. One in every five women in South Korea have had plastic surgery. When one looks at the 30- to 39-year-old group, 31% of women have gone under the knife, and those statistics are nearly a decade old.[3] I don't mean to pick on just one country, because many people around the world, from many different countries and cultures, are not satisfied with their looks. I myself have had plenty of times when I wished my body were different.

While we are talking about your body, we can't leave out the fact that you have your unique identifying markers. I'm talking about the fact that you have your fingerprints which are different from anyone else's. They serve as your personal "barcode." And that's literally true these days, as you likely use your fingerprint to open your phone, access your bank app, and get into your safe deposit box. Did you realize your fingerprints remain unchanged from the way they formed from the time you were a fetus until you die? Amazingly, despite any damage the skin may suffer, your fingerprints are always regenerated following the original pattern. They are yours forever and yours alone, as long as you are in this life. Plus, you have your DNA. The full readout of your DNA, your genome, is yours alone. A single strand of DNA is thousands of times thinner than a single strand of human hair, and yet it resides in every cell of your body, and it contains an astounding amount of complex information. Most of your DNA is the same as that of every other human being, but there is a micro portion of your DNA that is unique to you and makes you different from all the other eight billion human beings on the planet. Your DNA is yours alone.

While DNA is an individual matter, some things that

are yours have to do with other people. We're talking here about your relationships. Some of them might be a source of joy, and some of them may bring pain into your life. In some cases, you wouldn't know what to do *without* your relationships, and in other cases you don't know what to do *with* your relationships. But for good or for ill, they are *your* relationships, and you have to figure out how to enjoy them and nurture them, and how to navigate through them, around them, and in them—or perhaps how to get out of them. Before this book is done, we'll have more significant things to say about your relationships.

Finally, before we leave the word *your*, let me mention one you, on your own, might overlook: your worldview. I am guessing that you don't use the word *worldview* very often. It probably didn't come up the last time you were with friends. You may never use it, but I am talking here about how you see life: its purpose, its meaning. It's how you see the world and your place in it. Your worldview will determine your priorities, values, and goals. This is very closely related to your belief system. Maybe there's no difference. You might not be all that aware of what your worldview is, but I encourage you to take some time to look for it. Even though your worldview may fly under the radar of your everyday thinking, it has a powerful effect. Perhaps part two of this book will help you reshape it.

"Your" represents parts of your life—some difficult and some refreshing, some routine and some exhilarating, some problematic and some enjoyable—but the word *your* is a reminder that you have been given a big package of life and now it's your choice. In the words of Mary Oliver, "What is it you plan to do with *your* one wild and precious life?"

Chapter 2

One

What can we say about the word *one*? In her poetic line, Mary Oliver uses the word to emphasize that we have only a singular life to work with. We have one go-round. We don't get to live two or three and then, and then pick the one with the highest score.

Recently, I watched a basketball game, and at halftime, a fan was given one chance to make a shot from half-court in order to win a pile of money. He missed. But at halftime of another game, a student had one chance to make a golf putt that would have to travel all the way across the basketball court from goal to goal—a ninety-four-foot putt, not on a green but on a hardwood floor! He just was given one try. Miraculously, he "sank" the putt. That's what we might call a "one and done" event. You get one try. No mulligans. Would you say life is a lot like that?

In some ways I would say yes; in some ways no. You and I have a lot longer to work on our life than those guys. Their tries were over in a couple of seconds; life unfolds over a broad span of time. In your one life, there will be different chapters and maybe different opportunities to make changes, but when it comes to an end, and you don't like the outcome, you don't get a do-over. You're going to live your one life, and that will be it. It will be one and done. I am not a believer in reincarnation or in parallel universes.

During my life I have had three children, multiple houses (but not at the same time!), multiple motor vehicles, several sets of golf clubs, at least four tennis rackets, and on we could go. As a dedicated bibliophile, in my life I've had many books. After simplifying, in order to make numerous moves, I have far less today, but I still have many books. However, I have one that is very special. It is my one book personally autographed in my presence by a renowned scholar. You may have a priceless keepsake in your possession. It likely has some important sentimental value. You have nothing else like it, and you would not want to lose it. If you had to exit for a fire alarm, it would be one of the items you would grab as you dashed out the door. It is one of a kind, irreplaceable, priceless. As I see it, that is a bit like you and me: We are one of a kind, and we are valuable, priceless, and we get to take this singular, unique life and do something worthwhile with it.

In your one life, you will make a lot of different decisions and go in a lot of different directions. In that sense, sometimes it may feel like you are living several different lives. Now that I've reached my upper-seventies, I sometimes refer to things that happened to me years ago as being a part of "another lifetime," because it almost feels that way. But the Tom who did things many years ago was the same Tom of today—same fingerprints, same DNA. All part of my one life.

And it is quite enough that I only have one life because this one life has such great value. If you were to see me in a crowd, I would just be another old white guy blending in with a lot of other old white guys, but no one else has had my one life. I discovered recently that a famous fiction writer and I were born on exactly the same day. Some people would say that puts us under the same zodiac sign. But we could not be more different and the lives we have lived could not be more different. His is unique and mine is unique. And yours is unique. No one else has your one life.

When we have only one of a particular item, we are usually very careful with it. If I've only got enough coffee for one cup, I am strategic and intentional about when to drink that coffee. When we only have one shot left on a roll of film, we are very careful about... Let's scratch that, most of us don't take photos that way anymore. But you get the idea. And so it is with life. We get one life. But the one life we get is full of specialness and uniqueness and value. It is one that must not be wasted. It calls for a plan and for intentionality.

One. One chance. One shot. One life.

"What is it you plan to do with your one wild and precious life?"

Chapter 3

Wild

This word *wild* drew me to Mary Oliver's poem more than anything else. "Your one wild and precious life." Without the word *wild*, I don't think she would have hooked me.

There is something about the word wild that just has an attraction. There's something romantic-sounding about the Wild West and something exciting about the wild outdoors. When John Eldridge wrote his book *Wild at Heart*, the very title, and all it represented, resonated with men who were longing for more in their lives.[4] As of the time of this writing, the Goodreads website lists 714 books with the word *wild* in the title. Its magnetic quality is obvious to many.

Why does the word *wild* have such drawing power? I recently read an article touting the power of words in retail. It advised salespeople to use these six words or phrases: *new, free, because, instant, how to,* and *you*. The same site went on to give a number of what it called "greed-based power words," words like *lucrative* and *wealth*. I didn't see *wild* anywhere on the list. I guess the idea of wildness doesn't appeal in certain fields. (Who wants a wild experience with a dishwasher, TV or minivan?) Nevertheless, I still think the word has a lot of drawing power.

Now, I can't pretend to tell you that I know exactly what Mary Oliver meant when she used the word *wild*, but I can tell you the way I'm thinking about it, and you'll need to know this to continue on our ride.

When we go to *dictionary.com*, we find eighteen definitions for our word "wild." That fact itself is wild, given that definition number 13 is "amazing or incredible."[15] But combine that with the fact that on the Miriam Webster website you find at least additional definitions for the same word:[6]

1. Filled with many twists and turns: "a wild ride down the mountain"

2. Marked by turbulent agitation: "a wild and stormy night"

3. Deviating from the intended or expected course: "a wild White House press conference"

Life unfolds in unpredictable, sometimes overwhelming, ways. You may feel like you are holding on to the roller coaster car for dear life. You make a slow climb to the top and then comes a big drop, diving into a sharp curve, and then a little flat spot, and then another drop before another rise.

Life can be wild. For most of us, there will be some twists and turns, some bumpy spots, and some turbulence: That sense of value you feel when someone notices and affirms your work—you are on the upswing. That feeling of panic when the doctor says the word *cancer*—down you go. That feeling of shock when you discover a friend has betrayed you—whoa, into a big curve. The long-awaited news that you are being promoted and you're getting a big raise—up you go. The joy you have when you make the team—up. The disappointment when the college admissions email arrives: "Sorry, not accepted"—down. The deep and relentless grief of losing someone you love—down, way down.

The joy of having family together again and the endorphins start flowing from all those hugs—up. The euphoric joy of a wedding day—up. The pain of an unproductive conversation; the door slams and you don't know where he is going—down, down.

A wild ride.

When I write of "wild," I am thinking of someone

like James, who says, "I have had a wild week," and is referring to how his car stopped running, he broke a tooth while nibbling on a potato chip and his boss asked him to take an unpaid leave for the next six weeks. All this just a month after his girlfriend agreed to marry him and they had formulated a tight but doable financial plan leading up to the wedding.

I am thinking of someone like Maria, who was on her way to receive an award at work when her three-year-old started projectile vomiting from the back seat, which led to her being stopped by the police for erratic driving. Before she could clean up her son and get to the award ceremony, she was called to the hospital because her eighty-four-year-old grandmother had just had a stroke. "It's been wild," she says.

When I think of *wild*, I'm also thinking about some of you parents who have kids involved in sports, music, drama, and more. It is hard for me to keep track of all the things my one granddaughter, who is only in the third grade, is involved in. Her parents drive her everywhere, even as they juggle work and Christian ministry. Whenever I talk to my daughter or her husband, I'm reminded of how wild their lives can be. And they have only one child.

When I think of *wild*, I think of people I know who work two or three jobs. Somewhere in that packed schedule, they are trying to find time to sleep, often not successfully. They have no paid vacation time, and so they keep up this wild schedule year-round without a break. They don't want to work this much; they are just trying to make ends meet. When I think about keeping that schedule and handling that pressure, it seems overwhelming. And that's the thing about *wild*: sometimes it's fun and exciting; other times it's spirit-crushing.

My Wild Ride

When I think about wild times in my life, I think about being thirty-three years old. As my wife and I were preparing for our third child to have open-heart surgery to correct a serious birth defect, I was fired from a ministry job I had held for nine years. The church leadership could not have been more complimentary of our work, but they felt the controversy around it was much too risky. To add to the wildness of the ride, just days after I got fired, our house also got fired... as in, it literally caught fire. We had to move into a borrowed house for six weeks while we looked for new employment. At the same time, I was going from doctor to doctor, trying to get answers for some strange things that were happening in my body. Oh, and while we were living in that temporary housing, my wife and sick daughter caught a severe strain of the flu, which caused more flu-related deaths than the U.S. had seen in the previous twenty-two years. My wife and daughter lay ill for more than a week, during which time southwest Missouri was hit by the largest snowstorm in a decade. We were trapped for three days. It seemed to be a wild ride.

Six months later, with our daughter doing well after her dangerous surgery, we moved to a new city and new congregation, where we were welcomed with open arms. Over the next year, we saw fifty people from twelve nations become disciples of Jesus. We saw a spiritual resurgence in a small town in northeast Missouri. In the midst of all this, I was diagnosed with multiple sclerosis. Yes, it was wild! Now 44 years later, at 77, I find life to be as wild as ever. I have just moved for the fourth time in thirteen months!

Wild... and Messy

The wild ride sometimes takes you to some dark places. I have not been on an amusement park ride in many years, but in the 1970s I rode a ride called "Fire in the Hole" at Silver Dollar City in Branson, Missouri. Fire in the Hole was an indoor roller coaster that hurled riders up and down and sideways through some spooky darkness simulating working in a mine. Similarly, some of our wild times in life are also dark times. They may be so difficult they leave scars. We may come out of the darkness, but the darkness may continue to follow us and even become part of our ride.

After reading Mary Oliver's poem and starting to think about a book inspired by her words, my early thought was to change her words a bit and write about our "messy and magnificent life." Because not only is life wild; it's also messy. One of the definitions of *wild* had to do with being out of control and unruly. That gets us into the ballpark of *messy*.

We have mentioned relationships and how they are important but can also be challenging. They can sometimes get tangled and complicated—really messy—and it can be hard to know how to clean them up. Sorting out conflict and misunderstanding can make a mess in the middle of your already-wild ride.

Wild, unpredictable, complicated, messy. That is often the nature of life. Years ago, my wife and I went out to dinner one night with a whole group of friends to celebrate someone's birthday. We went to a Chinese restaurant and so when they brought the fortune cookies, everyone was asked to read the little paper and then add "in the bathroom." So, you got things like:

–A new pair of shoes will do you a world of good. In the bathroom.

–A thrilling time is in your immediate future. In the bathroom.

—Avoid taking unnecessary gambles. In the bathroom.

—Your road to glory will be rocky but fulfilling. In the bathroom.

—Patience is your ally at the moment. Don't worry. In the bathroom.

—Don't pursue happiness. Create it. In the bathroom.

After that hilarious activity, I couldn't help but think how many important lessons I have actually learned in the bathroom. In my earlier days with MS, I was one of a number of people in my circle who began some alternative medicine treatments. One of the routines that everyone in this program was on was... get ready... daily coffee enemas. For almost a year, every day I was not only in the bathroom, but I was on the floor in the bathroom. Now out of respect for the TMI thing, I won't go any further. I will just say that life gets messy—literally and figuratively—and I have learned a lot of lessons in the bathroom. I spent a lot of time alone in bathrooms, which, oddly enough, gave me extra quiet time for prayer.

Sometimes we are tempted to hide from others how messy our life is. We want our lives to look orderly and under control. Now that I'm seventy-seven and not thirty-seven or forty-seven, I no longer try to hide that my life is messy. (Well, not as often as I used to, anyway.) When I was younger, I wanted to keep up a good front and act like I had my life together. But MS and some long bouts of depression tore down my exterior appearances, exposing the ways I did not "have it together." I ended up writing a book titled *Mind Change,* in which I was honest about the mess my mind could get in. But I was also able to share how I found some answers in the middle of my mess.

I recently watched a movie called *Everything Everywhere All at Once.* The movie gives a new definition to "a wild ride" as the characters jump from one parallel universe to another, trying to manage their lives. Maybe the more academic word for "a wild ride" is "complexity," and this movie had plenty of it. Thankfully, you and I only live in one universe (that we are aware of); each of us must learn how to live in the chaos, to hold on and find what is valuable and special.

Yes, life is wild, complex, sometimes messy, sometimes dark but often exhilarating, And thankfully sometimes quiet and serene. What is your plan, the poet asks. "What is it you plan to do with your one wild and precious life?"

Chapter 4

Precious

It's a good thing Mary Oliver used the word *wild*, because the word *precious* would not have grabbed me. But "wild and precious" has a good ring to it, a sort of yen and yang character. When you hear the word *precious,* what are your first thoughts? My mind goes to the ubiquitous Precious Moments figurines, featuring cute children with teardrop-shaped eyes. Those little figurines made their appearance in 1978 and took the 1980s by storm. In 1998, the *Chicago Tribune* reported that more than two million wedding cakes had been topped with Precious Moments bride and groom figurines. Obviously, a lot of people found them precious. Twenty-five years later they are still selling, with an exploding product extension, and there is even a Precious Moments Museum somewhere in Missouri.

Maybe the word *precious* brings to mind the character Gollum in *The Lord of the Rings*. Can you hear his gravelly voice? "We wants it, we needs it. Must have the precious. They stole it from us. Sneaky little hobbitses. Wicked, tricksy, false!" Gollum was talking, of course, about the ring, but coming out of his mouth, the word does not sound so precious.

Precious. I think of adorable pictures I see on social media of babies and toddlers and how often people comment, "Precious." Although precious is not a word I use very often, when my daughter would send me pictures of my granddaughter when she was a tiny tyke, I often texted back, "Precious." It just seemed to be the right word. What was I trying to say? Sometimes I meant "so cute." But it was more than cute—I saw a sweetness and an innocence. Her expression, her presence, were treasures to hold on to. I think that is getting to one meaning of *precious*.

While precious describes that which is adorable, cuddly and loveable, it also shows up in the hard cold world of business and commerce as investors keep an eye on the changing prices of precious metals: gold, silver, platinum, and others. They are precious because they are rare and are of great value. Then similarly, you have the precious jewels: the diamond, the pearl, the ruby, the sapphire, the emerald, the alexandrite and the cat's-eye chrysobery. No, I had not heard of those last two either.

I think I've read enough of Mary Oliver's poetry, and enough of what others have to say about her and her work, to have a pretty good idea of what she means when she uses the word *precious*. Mary had the ability to spend time in this world with her eyes open and to be constantly captivated by the gift of life we have all been given. She seemed to see what many of us are too busy to see. I can tell she thought that every life is valuable because every life can see and take in all the amazing elements of our world if one will but slow down and pay attention. That is the reason every life is precious like a precious stone.

For sure, there are many things in this world that are not marvelous and wonderful. There is pain and ugliness and tragedy. The concentration camps in the Second World War had to be the most horrible environment human beings could ever experience. But even there, such people as Viktor Frankl, Corrie ten Boom and Fania Fénelon found light, beauty and meaning. That is further testimony to how precious life is. Every life.

There is an old Christian hymn that says, "This world is not my home; I'm just a-passin' thru, my treasures are laid up somewhere beyond the blue."[7] For a long time I found that hymn to be a fun song and mildly comforting. In 1961 there was a musical that came to Broadway titled *Stop the World. I Want to Get Off,* and there certainly days that you feel like that. But I have changed my mind about that hymn and decided that the writer got it wrong. Right now, this planet is our home, the place where we get to live our one wild life. This is the place and time we get to appreciate how precious life is. I don't buy the idea that this world and this life are all there is. I am convinced we can look forward to a much-enhanced version of life in a coming age, but still make it our first order of business to appreciate and be in awe of the life we have now.

So, what will you do? Will you just use your life to merely visit this world, or will you treat life as a precious gift, a pearl of great value, something priceless to be embraced?

Again, I ask, with Mary, "What is it you plan to do with your one wild and precious life?"

Chapter 5

Life

We've already had a lot to say about life. And we've just mainly been dealing with the adjectives! So, what is true about the noun *life* that we haven't already discussed? Well, there are some more matters we need to look at.

I frequently read the columns of a widely-read and articulate woman who is a skeptic when it comes to faith. So, I was stunned when she recently wrote, "It's a miracle that we're even here at all." I imagine she's referring to the fact that, naturally speaking, the ridiculous odds were against human life ever existing. In an online article titled "The Chance Events that Led to Human Existence," another essayist with the BBC writes that we have, surprisingly, ended up with "a universe with exactly the right constants of nature to create the conditions for life. A human universe."[8] That is not the first article of this nature that I've read coming from a scientific point of view. (It is interesting to me that people can believe in the miracle and not in the miracle maker, but that's a subject for another day.)

When you nerd out on this topic, you'll see how much the odds were against life, and then how the odds were even greater against the development of intelligence. As she said, "It's a miracle that we're even here at all." Some people think as she does—they don't believe in miracles—but we are all living one every day! Life itself is a miracle. By the way, if you want to have your mind blown and have some fun, just do some research about the finger monkey, also known as Pygmy marmosets. Weighing in at just over 100 g (3.5 oz), they will amaze you. But then stand in awe of a planet full of such incredible creatures.

Right now, there are eight billion of us humans on this planet. From the thirty-thousand-foot view, we may all look the same, but the closer you get and the more carefully you examine us, the more you see that each individual life is different from all the other lives. And that's true, as mentioned earlier, even in the case of identical twins or identical triplets. Each one is distinct, unique. That means you are amazing, whatever you may feel about yourself.

You Have a Choice

What is your plan for your life? Mary Oliver's question assumes that in life you have a choice. And that is something else amazing about you. You have a choice, and you are the one who gets to make it. You didn't have a choice about when you were born or who your parents would be or who would be in your family. But now that you've arrived, you get to look at options for many aspects of how you live your life. You get to check out different plans. And then you have a choice.

A few years ago, I was enrolled in the Medicare system, the medical insurance we have in the United States for seniors. Suddenly I began to receive countless offers for different companies wanting to sign me up in their "Medicare advantage plans." The plans can be quite different. I had to look them over and make a choice of which plan I wanted. So it is with your life. There are a lot of plans out there. Some are prepackaged, and you can almost buy them off the shelf. But you can also start from scratch and completely make up your own. You have a lot of different choices. But what plan do you choose?

Chances are, some of you are pretty far down the road with a life plan. But the amazing thing about this life we are given is that you can choose to change plans. There's an old word that some people think is just for religion: *repentance*. Repentance basically means a decision to change your plan. We may think of repentance as a decision to stop some singular bad behavior, but its real meaning refers to a much larger transformation. It is like you've been moving with one big plan, but then you stop and reevaluate and decide a new plan is needed. We will come back to repentance later, but that's one of the outrageous things Jesus offered: a new plan. But I don't want to run ahead.

All of us have heard the expression, "Think for yourself." One of the most amazing things about your life is that you can do that. Each of us gets to choose what life we want to live. We get to choose those things we're going to set our mind on, those things we are going to pursue. Even people seemingly trapped in an addiction are taught, as they go through treatment, that they still have a choice.

I can almost hear some of you saying, *Maybe I am amazing, but I'm not happy with the amazing person I am. I don't really like being me.* Let me tell you another amazing thing: You have the freedom to escape those thoughts. You have the freedom to give up the thought-plan you are currently following that involves feeding yourself more and more negativity.

You are amazing. Please believe me. "No, no," you say, "I am just an ordinary guy from the Midwest," or

"I'm just an ordinary woman from New York" or "I'm just an ordinary person in Seattle or Taipei," or "No, no, I'm just a domestic worker... bus driver... restaurant server." But you are not ordinary. You are unique. You are the company owner of yourself. You are amazing.

But wait. Don't get puffed up. No chest-beating. No trash-talking. I didn't say you had earned your way to your amazing status. It's very important that you never forget that. Your amazing status was given to you as a gift, and you get to use it to honor whomever you want to honor. You may use it to honor your own amazing self or you might take a more humble approach realizing the gift was given to you for something greater.

You do have a choice. You can choose to hold onto your life, or you can choose to give control to someone else. So can I. I can choose to keep control of my company, *Tom A. Jones, Inc.*, or give the control over to someone else. You can sign your plan over to the military or to a corporation or to another person or some charismatic religious leader, but even then, down the line, you can choose to switch plans. It may get more difficult the more deeply you have ensconced yourself in something, but you can still change plans. And even if you get involved in a plan that's not so great, and you get knocked down by the whole experience, you are still amazing.

Years ago, shortly after moving from Boston to Tennessee, my wife and I were in our front yard and one of our neighbors, who was about our age, went zooming by on her bicycle, leaning into the curve at the end of our street. I said to Sheila, "Peggy is amazing." Then as those of us with disabilities tend to do, I thought, "But I can't do that. I will never ride a bicycle again." But then, thankfully, I didn't let my thoughts end there. I knew I had the ability to think something else, and so I made a mind change and asked myself, "Why don't you be the most amazing person that uses an electric scooter? Not everybody gets the chance to do that, but you have a chance to be that person." (Now, on most days, I'm using an electric wheelchair. But the principal remains the same).

That's how amazing we all are. I'm unique, but not in the sense of being the only one who can do certain things. All of us have that amazing capacity when it comes to our life. We get to determine what our life is going to be focused on. That was the idea in the book I wrote more thirty years ago, *Mind Change*. You can change your mind just as you can change your plan.

Your Amazing Mind

Let's take a moment to consider the human mind. The mind truly deserves the word "amazing." Have you ever stopped to think about how many things our minds do just to get us ready to leave the house each day? Think about all the things you remember to do to get ready, and all the things your mind remembers to take with you—and you haven't even set one foot out the door yet! Amazing.

Even as you are reading this book, your mind can turn on a dime and focus in many different directions. You can stop reading, close your eyes for a minute, and start making lists of seven things you need to do, or five people you appreciate, or three vacation spots you might visit five months from now. Or you can think back to when you were age ten, and you can see your childhood bedroom, and you can mentally walk through the house you lived in and remember so many details. Now that I have mentioned the idea, you're probably doing it right now.

Your mind did all those things without turning on a device, without getting on the Internet, without plugging anything in or replacing any batteries. To say that the human mind is amazing doesn't even tell the half of it. Even if you feel like you're starting to lose yours, what you have left is probably still amazing. I grant you that some minds, like those of Marie Curie, Albert Einstein, and Stephen Hawking, are off the charts. But *all* of us have a prodigious number of little gray cells up there—as in, about ninety billion—that cause us to have amazing minds too.

Part of the reason some people don't make better decisions about life may be that they don't appreciate how amazing and precious their minds, and lives really are. So, if you weren't sure where this book is going, it has become clear at least one place it needed to go, and that is to convince you that you are amazing and have an amazing life. Be in awe.

You may just now be graduating from high school or from college. You might be sitting in incarceration. You might be working a factory job. You might be in a corner office running a big company. You may have just gone through a painful relationship split. You may have just made some big mistakes that are haunting you. You might be in your seventies, no longer able to drive, living in a senior housing facility. You may spend most of your day serving as the caregiver for a loved one. But if you can understand the words you are reading, your mind is still amazing. If you can be convinced of that, then a world of possibilities is still open to you.

My wife was a huge fan of birds, and because of her, I came to have a great appreciation for avian life. Almost twenty years ago we watched a BBC documentary series called *The Life of Birds,* narrated by the great David Attenborough. That show proved to me that birds are incredible, sometimes leaving me absolutely gobsmacked. But hear me clearly: Your life is even more amazing than the life of birds. So, we could actually add a word to Mary Oliver's question, "What is it you plan to do with your one *amazing,* wild and precious life?"

Now I grant you, amazing is not the only thing you are. Have I built you up too much? Just in case, let me remind you that you are also weak and far from perfect. You do not have superpowers, and even if you have big muscles, there are still chinks in your armor. In our amazing lives we have strengths, and we have weaknesses. Now, you can focus on those weaknesses and get yourself in a state of helplessness. Or you can recognize those weaknesses, be honest about them, and find resources that help you overcome them. Your weaknesses don't have to define you or rule you. What a life you have!

But in case I'm not being clear enough, there is something else we need to do. We need to stand in *awe* at the gift of life we've been given. We use the word *awesome* often in our culture, but do we really experience the "awe" part? When is the last time you were in awe? You know, you don't have to go to the Grand Canyon to be in awe. Or to Niagara Falls or to the Great Pyramid of Giza. You don't have to look through the new Webb telescope. You can simply look at the incredible gift of life we have been given, and be in awe. And that might very well mean standing in a state of inspired humility.

One reviewer called Mary Oliver "the poet of awe."[9] Mary once wrote, "Attention is our endless and proper work."[10] And when she paid attention to what was around her, she stood in awe. She could be fascinated by a grasshopper sitting on her hand and looking up at her with its big eyes. She could be captivated by the wind, the wildflowers or the catbird. We have each been given a life. Are we paying attention? Do we stand in awe? Tell me, what is it you plan to do with your one wild and precious and awesome and amazing life? Oliver ends another poem of hers with these words: "Here you are, alive. Would you like to make a comment?"[11]

Part 2

Chapter 6

Outrageous

We are going to shift gears a bit. Did I warn you that this book is going to be a wild ride? To start this new part, I need to tell you about a boy named Asher. Asher grew up many years ago in a small town in northern Palestine, or you could say where modern Israel is today. The town was called Mizra. So he was known as Asher of Mizra. Now, if you had grown up in Mizra, you probably wouldn't have thought there was anything all that special about Asher. However, his parents knew there was something unique about him—but don't a lot of parents think there's something special about their kids?

Asher went to school and most likely worked in his father's butcher's shop, and from all we can tell, he didn't create much of a stir until he was around thirty years old. But suddenly he broke his silence and he was out there among the people saying things and doing things that were, in the words of some people, "remarkable" and "astonishing." And yes, he was saying and doing some things that were outrageous—so outrageous that the people of Mizra took him out to the edge of town and tried to throw him out to either get rid of him or kill him. And that was just after his first sermon.

From this most interesting beginning, Asher went on to become infamous in the eyes of some community leaders. He started a gang, or at least that's what some people said, and his band wandered around from town to town, turning a lot of things upside down—or so it seemed to the people in charge, who finally decided to take action. I am really condensing the story here, but Asher was put on trial and then, of all things, he was publicly executed. His mother was there when he died.

But then after a month or so, all this talk started, with some saying Asher was alive. More and more people reported this shocking news, and all kinds of people from all walks of life decided to follow his teachings in spite of the fact that they seemed outrageous.

Well, maybe you're catching on. The boy's name was Yeshua or Jesus, not Asher, and the city he grew up in was called Nazareth, not Mizra. And his father was a carpenter, not a butcher. I changed the names and details, just for a few paragraphs, because I didn't want you to hear the name "Jesus" and think, "Oh, I already know this story," and immediately stop reading.

But what I want to do is introduce your wild and precious life to the outrageous Jesus, and I want to invite you into some conversation. Maybe when we began, you didn't know how precious your life is, and maybe you still don't know how outrageous Jesus is. But I think some very interesting things could happen when we bring those two truths together. That's what I was thinking when I first conceived this book.

As a writer, I'm always thinking about the message I want to convey, but I'm also thinking about the possible resistances I could face, and so let me tell you several things I'm thinking about: First, I bet some of you think you already know a lot about Jesus, and you don't think there's anything all that outrageous about him. Ask the average Christian believer to name three or four qualities of Jesus, and "outrageous" would not be one of the popular choices! Ask the same question to people who don't follow Jesus, and you might get different answers, but still it's unlikely the word *outrageous* would come up. Regardless of your background, you probably have some innate resistance to thinking of Jesus in this way, just as you wouldn't want to say Moses, Buddha, or Muhammad were outrageous. Maybe you've got a lot of other boxes you would put Jesus in, but *outrageous* would not be one of them. So much of the world, including the religious part of it, has done quite a job of thoroughly domesticating Jesus. If your view of Jesus is bland and vanilla—decidedly "un-outrageous"—I hope to convince you otherwise.

Second, I know I could get some pushback because Jesus lived a long time ago. Maybe he did a good job of addressing the wild and precious life of people back then, but we live in a different time. Historians generally consider anything before 500 A.D. to be ancient—and Jesus lived more than two thousand years ago! So, what can a man who lived in such ancient times possibly have to say to someone who lives in our modern world?

The third reason I think some of you might be pulling back a little bit is that my enthusiasm for Jesus sounds a little like a bad movie you've seen before. Somewhere along the line you went to church and they talked a lot about Jesus, and they sang songs like, "Oh, How I Love Jesus," but you didn't see much that interested you, and you didn't notice any dramatic changes in people's lives. In fact, it seemed like for some of them, their religion was doing more harm than good. So now you basically have a feeling of, "I've been there, done that, and it's not for me." You feel that Jesus has been tried and found wanting.

Fourth, I think some small number of you think Jesus *is* outrageous—and a bit dangerous, just as people thought in his own day. You know enough about him to feel he's a threat to your life—your life that you are fond of and think is pretty good. You suspect that getting involved with him could really upset the apple cart of your life. You would rather keep your distance. But since by some miracle you have come this far in this short book, don't you want to see if there's something outrageous about Jesus that you don't know or that you might need to hear?

I could be completely wrong. Maybe none of you have any resistance but are ready to move on and hear the rest of the story. But if I've described some of your hesitations, I want to encourage you to press on through your reluctance, open your eyes, open your mind, and see if it makes any difference as we try to confront the reality of Jesus.

Outrageously Good?

There are all kinds of ways to be outrageous. Most of them are not good. In fact, I am hard-pressed to come up with any examples of the word *outrageous* being used in a positive sense. Being a man of my times, of course, I had to stop and do an Internet search of "outrageously good," and mostly what I found were foods—everything from "outrageously good" vegan spinach artichoke dip to "outrageously good" oatmeal raisin cookies. (You can take a snack break right now if I'm making you hungry.) Still, outside a few exciting snacks, the word *outrageous* is reserved mostly for things that are problems.

As I'm writing these words, the news is full of stories about a newly-elected U.S. congressman from New York state, George Santos. After the election, it was revealed that almost everything on his résumé was a lie. Santos claimed he was Jewish, that his mother died in the 9/11 attacks, and that he had graduated from a prestigious university and then worked for two prominent Wall Street firms. None of those things were true. And it turned out those lies were only the beginning. After refusing to resign, he was eventually expelled from the House of Representatives. It would be hard to count the number of times the word *outrageous* has been used to describe his behavior.

I think of an outstanding wide receiver in the National Football League, a nine-year veteran, who went to the Pro Bowl seven times and won the Super Bowl. He got so frustrated during a game in 2022 that he went over to the sidelines, took off his jersey, his pads, and his undershirt. After throwing them all into the crowd, he jogged out of the stadium, shirtless, encouraging the fans to applaud. People called his behavior outrageous.

He was let go by his team the same week.

If you do a web search for our word, you might find stories of radio personalities, comedians, or even podcasters who draw their audiences by seeking to be more outrageous than others. You might find a story about "The Naked Cowboy," who has been playing the guitar and singing in his underwear for the last twenty-five years in Times Square in all kinds of weather. New Yorkers have gotten so used to him that he may no longer fit the "outrageous" category.

Your search might bring up something about the Netflix series *Tiger King*. The show featured Joe Exotic, who owned a private zoo with big cats. One media writer observed, "Let's face it: It's impossible to look away from people like [him], even if you don't particularly like him or his behavior. He's loud, takes up a ton of space, loves to self-promote and is so shockingly outlandish. He has a psychological allure that's hard to ignore."[12] Thirty-four million people watched the series in its first ten days, a Netflix record. People just couldn't look away. Turns out that some of what Joe did was not only outrageous but illegal. He is currently serving a twenty-two-year prison sentence.

Given these examples, it may not seem wise to talk about Jesus' outrageousness. If, after you read this book, you want to correct me, honestly, I will listen.

However, there's something about the word that gets at how drastically different and shocking the life and message of Jesus were. So, for now, I am sticking with it, and I hope in the coming pages to help you not only see why I consider Jesus outrageous, but also why his outrageousness matters.

Quietly, Righteously, Lovingly Outrageous

Behavior can be outrageous because it is extremely wrong. You can do things that are shockingly obnoxious. You can cross many lines and be offensive, you can dress in ostentatious ways that draw attention to yourself. Of course, none of this is what makes Jesus outrageous.

"Outrageous" can also mean "unusual in such a way that it brings shock or surprise." or "very bold, unusual, and startling." Now there is a box that Jesus checked. Jesus' teachings went so much against the grain that they were considered shocking and surprising—in other words, outrageous. Jesus was not showy, flamboyant, reckless or deceptive, but he did leave people wide-eyed and slack-jawed, asking themselves some hard questions.

Some people are obnoxiously outrageous, but Jesus was quietly outrageous. He didn't go out in the middle of the streets raving and ranting (although he did once turn over some tables in the temple market to make a dramatic point). He was remarkable, unconventional, perplexing, unorthodox, extraordinary, unique, and bewildering. Some people thought he was insane, and others thought he was blasphemous. He was neither. There was no one else like him. He said things about himself and his relationship with God that were different from what any Jew before him had ever said. Other would-be messiahs showed up on the Jewish scene, but Jesus is the only one the people turned over to their enemies to be executed. That would seem to give further evidence for his outrageousness, at least in their eyes.

Maybe it was not possible for anyone else to be outrageous the way Jesus was. In his case, it almost seemed like he was from another world. Maybe that explains it. But what about you? Could you ever trust someone who is considered dangerous by others? Could you trust someone who has been labeled as outrageous? Well, the reality is, you shouldn't—at least not until you've taken a closer look. That is what we will try to do as you make your plan for your one wild and precious life.

Chapter 7

Insanely Generous

On Valentine's Day, 1990, the Voyager 1 space probe, after exploring planets for more than twelve years, was 3.7 billion miles from Earth and about to leave our solar system. Astronomer and author Carl Sagan made a special request to NASA, asking them to turn the camera on the spacecraft around and take one last picture of Planet Earth (yes, from almost four billion miles away). As I write these words, I am looking across the room at a framed copy of that picture, which I bought five years ago. From where I'm sitting, the picture looks like a mistake. The large picture is mostly black with a faint yellow streak, but if you get close enough to it you can see a tiny little speck of blue down in the bottom right quadrant. That is Planet Earth, and four years later Carl Sagan named the photo "The Pale Blue Dot."

Was God behind this? Jesus thought so

Looking at that tiny speck hanging there in the vast expanse of space brings to mind some of humankind's oldest questions: Who are we? Why are we here? Did some absolutely random coincidence bring about our universe and our little spot in it? Or is there some kind of a plan? And if there is a plan, does it follow that there is a God? And if there is a God, what is she or he or they like?

Jesus had a lot to say about that last question. He talked a lot about God and about what God is like. He said things about God and told stories about God that had shocking implications. Some people, even some great thinkers, have thought very highly of Jesus, considering him a great teacher or brilliant sage, but they have tried to disconnect him from all talk of things divine or supernatural. One of the most famous proponents of this perspective was our third American president, Thomas Jefferson. He decided to take his physical copy of the New Testament and remove all the "unscientific" references to divine things, especially miracles, so that he could end up with a collection of Jesus' moral teachings.

In Jefferson's own words, found in a letter to another former president, John Adams, he described his process: "I have performed this operation for my own use, by cutting verse by verse out of the printed book, and arranging the matter which is evidently [Jesus'], and which is as easily distinguishable as diamonds in a dunghill." Jefferson literally did a cut and paste job to create his own version of the Gospels. I imagine he ended up with a thin volume! No serious scholar today takes the so-called "Jefferson Bible" seriously, and the nation certainly didn't build a beautiful memorial to him among the cherry trees in Washington because of how he helped us understand Jesus. The "operation" on the Gospels was not his finest hour.

There is no way to separate who Jesus was, or what he taught, from his constant references to God. He tied everything he said to God, God's will, God's power, and, perhaps most of all, to God's love. Jesus was a Jew, living in a God-affirming culture, and his people had been hearing from Moses and the prophets for hundreds of years, and they were convinced that they had a very good idea of what God was like. The Jewish Scriptures described his steadfast love and did so again and again. In contrast to the gods of the nations around them, the God of Israel was described as committed to justice, but also full of mercy and kindness, especially for his people of the covenant. Despite the failings and shortcomings of his people, God remained faithful, compassionate, and merciful, continuously extending his love and grace toward them. So, in such a context, what did Jesus say about God's love that was so outrageous and astounding? We will be looking at some of these statements in this chapter and the next.

At this point, I want to mention my debt to another writer, a scholar and a novelist. I'll give him a proper introduction in the notes at the end of the book, but for now, I'm just going to call him Andy so as not to sound too formal or academic. When I first read Andy fifty-three years ago, I was struck by the fact that he said Jesus' message is saturated with *"the insanely generous love of God."*[5] The insanely generous love of God. That was a new phrase for me. It stuck in my mind, has stayed there ever since, and is the focus of this chapter.

A New View of God's Love

Before we plunge in, let's first get some additional context so we can appreciate the stunning nature of Jesus' teaching. The Jewish people believed God had promised them a messiah (a savior/king/ leader) and in the first century, they looked for this one to come leading a revolt against the Romans driving the hated occupiers out of their country. The more important context—perhaps we could call it the spiritual context—is that the Jews needed, along with the rest of the world, someone to deliver them from the spiritual mess they were in. Jesus had no interest in saving the Jews militarily; his primary focus was on saving them spiritually and bringing the reign of God into their lives.

Social science research tells us that almost no one thinks of themselves as a bad person, and even fewer think of themselves as immoral. Jesus came to save people who saw themselves as the good guys. For generations, the Jews had been told that they were God's chosen people, his children, and they felt good about their standing with God. So, when Jesus told them that they needed to be set free, you can imagine their confusion and annoyance: "They answered him, "We are Abraham's descendants and have never been slaves of anyone. How can you say that we shall be set free?"[16]

But Jesus was ushering in the kingdom of God, and he was exposing the fact that *everyone* was in a mess, including the Jewish people. *Everyone* needed deliverance into a whole new way of living: kingdom living. Jesus wanted the Jews—and all of us—to see that though we are all in a mess, there's something that can turn us completely around.

On one occasion Jesus said, "No one is good but God alone".[17] On another occasion he said, "Though you are evil, you give good gifts to all your children."[18] He frequently addressed the fact that there was sin, and there are sinners, and that sin is a problem. But

Jesus had a different take on all this. Although Jesus did expose sin, he didn't walk around passing judgment on everyone. He seldom condemned sin—unless it was the sin of self-righteousness and hypocrisy. In fact, Jesus was criticized for spending time with sinners. Somewhere I read recently about a woman in our day whose life had led her into prostitution, but then she started seeking solutions. Someone asked her if she had reached out to the church, and her comment was "Why would I go there? I already feel bad enough. Why would I go somewhere that would make me feel worse?" It was quite different with Jesus: People who saw their sin were drawn to him. They somehow realized that in the context of their sin and mess, he was bringing good news.

Jesus used the word *repent,* but coming from him it didn't sound like, "Stop being a bad person:" it sounded like, "Open yourself up to a whole new possibility." And the reason there was a new possibility was because Jesus taught that the love of God goes beyond anything we've imagined. On the one hand, Jesus tells us the truth about ourselves, but on the other hand, that truth is swallowed up in this message that Andy calls "the insanely generous love of God."[19]

The stories or parables that Jesus taught probably bring out this truth the most. In the parables of the lost sheep and the lost coin, you have a shepherd who leaves ninety-nine sheep unprotected in order to go in search of one lost sheep and a woman who loses a coin in her house and seems to go nuts looking for it. Then Andy comments, "Only a crazy shepherd or foolish housewife would act like this." However, when we dig into the meaning of Jesus' stories, we realize those characters represent the God who goes over the top to find us when we are lost, all because of his outrageous love. (By the way, how outrageous to depict God as a woman!)

We have maybe Jesus' most famous story also in that same chapter that begins with the religious leaders indicting him for spending too much time with sinners. It is known around the world as the Parable of the Prodigal Son. It might be the greatest story anyone ever told. It's the story of a father and two sons, and the younger son asks for his inheritance in advance. The father complies. The son takes his money, goes away and spends it in wild living until he's broke, broken, and literally living with pigs. You probably remember the rest of this story. At the end of his rope, in the worst place a kosher-keeping Jew could find himself, the young son comes to his senses, prepares a speech of apology, comes home, and gets ready to plead with his father to just give him a role like the servants. The father, who seems to be looking for his lost son, sees him while he is still a long way off. He *runs to meet him*, embraces him and kisses him, all before the boy can even give his speech. He soon orders a great feast to welcome him home. Here again I turn to some of Andy's thoughts:

> God's passion for his people is so great that he dispenses with normal canons of discretion and good taste in dealing with us. Only a slightly demented father would shower honor on him who was a wastrel. Jesus likens God to a father who can't stop thinking about his rebellious ingrate son though he has another son who's respectful and obedient...The loving father does not even give the prodigal son time to finish his nicely rehearsed statement of sorrow. The son barely has begun before he is embraced, clothed in a new robe and propelled into a festive banquet. The novel element in his good news was that God's love was so powerful that it pushed him to the point of insanity.[20]

The Jewish people had been taught that God was loving—but was he really *this* loving? This affectionate? This personal? As a young man coming around to give Jesus a look, I remember seeing a book titled *Will God Run?* The title was highlighting the fact that this parable is the only time in the Scriptures that we find God running. And where was he running? Toward a sinful, unworthy son. For many of Jesus' hearers, that had to be an outrageous thought. Here's Andy again:

> We are scandalized by such behavior on the part of God. Why does he not behave with more dignity and respectability? If we were in his position, we would have heard out the prodigal son and then told him to come back in a few weeks when we had made our decision.[21]

Another author named Henry (again, see the cast of characters at the end) wrote an entire book based on this parable of Jesus, and he concluded we should all realize that our true identity is "Beloved."[22] Once we understand that we are beloved, regardless of our flaws, mistakes, or shortcomings, we can begin a fulfilling life. We can only get to that point by encountering the outrageous love of God. The Gospel of John will give us that well-known statement that God so loved the world that he gave his only begotten son.[23] With an outrageous love, God came shockingly in human flesh, but when people only focused on the outrageousness but missed the love, they refused to receive him.

Although times have changed, for decades, American textbooks for English literature for high school students included the text of the famous sermon by Puritan preacher Jonathan Edwards, titled "Sinners in the Hands of an Angry God." In Edwards's defense, he did have much more to say about God than that, but, nevertheless, he preached that sermon and, sadly, just the title has left a remarkable impact on many people (including me as a teenager). The truth is, you could hardly find a statement more opposite that of the message of Jesus, particularly as seen in the story of the prodigal son where we find the sinner so warmly and affectionately embraced by the forgiving father. In that remarkable story we see the loving outrageousness of Jesus and his message. Are we paying attention? Are we standing in awe?

A Banquet for All

Jesus told many other parables, of course, but let me mention one in particular that Andy is fond of: the parable of the wedding banquet.[24] Here we have a king who invites guests to his son's wedding banquet (which apparently represents the kingdom of God that is breaking in), but they all make excuses and refuse to come. The king then invites anyone he can find, good and bad alike, to fill the banquet hall. The story is both a rebuke to those who did not accept God's invitation and a statement about how God throws open the doors to any who will come. Here is Andy's thought: "Jesus likens God to a rich host who opens the doors of the banquet hall to a menagerie of bag ladies and bums."[25]

Jesus modeled this teaching—this love—with his

life. He frequently interacted with and ministered to people who were considered outcasts or marginalized by society, such as tax collectors, prostitutes, lepers, wine-drinkers, Samaritans, Gentiles, and others who were just called "sinners." His willingness to associate with and help all kinds of outcasts showed that his message of God's over-the-top love and salvation was for everyone, regardless of their social status or perceived worth.

So, did Andy get it right? Does Jesus' message describe God's kingdom as a sphere of outrageous, "insanely generous love" for everyone? Is Henry right that we are all God's "beloved"? And do you think I am right in bringing this to your attention? Should we stand in awe of this kind of love?

Remember the photo of "The Pale Blue Dot" hanging out there in space, taken from almost four billion miles away? I think Andy, Henry and I all agree that there is a God who put it there, and he has a plan, and at the center of the plan is the insanely generous love of that God. Does that change your plan for your one wild and precious life?

Chapter 8

Abba? How Dare You?

The Jewish people were taught that God was loving, but they emphasized having great respect for him. They sought to appreciate the fact that God was the Almighty, and he was wholly "other" from them. Years ago, I met a Jewish man who had made the unusual move of becoming a Christian. His late father had been from Russia and, as I recall, lived near the Black Sea. The man—who was in his eighties when I met him—could remember his father making copies by hand of the Hebrew Scriptures. He told me how, each time his father came to the word for God, before he wrote it, he would put down his pen and go out and immerse himself in the sea—a ritual immersion Jews call a *mikveh*. Talk about a profound reverence for the name of God!

Even today, when you visit many Jewish websites,

you will find that each time they write the name of God, it will be as printed as "G-d" or as "Gd," out of reverence for God's name. In Jesus' time people did not want to say the name of God because of its holiness. So, in the Gospel of Matthew, which is written primarily for a Jewish audience, you will find euphemisms used for God's names (for example, the kingdom of God is most often referred to as the kingdom of heaven).

As we noted earlier, the message the Jews seemed to receive from the Old Testament was that God loved his people, but you should keep something of a healthy distance between yourself and God. That message had come through quite clearly with the way the Jews were instructed to regard the Holy of Holies, also called the Most Holy Place. This was the central room in the Jewish tabernacle, and later in the temple. To enter the Holy of Holies was to enter the very presence of God. Only one person could go into that space, and *he could only go in once a year*. The high priest would enter the Most Holy Place on Yom Kippur (the Day of Atonement) to offer sacrifices for the sins of the people. The idea that a rope would be tied around the ankle of the chief priest so that if he died, he could be pulled out of the sacred space is likely a myth, but it is no distortion to say that the Jews viewed coming into the presence of God with a holy fear.

The Way Jesus Talked to God

When Jesus began teaching, the people had to be more than surprised to hear him constantly referring to God as his Father. Addressing God in such a casual and familiar way must have made most Jewish people uncomfortable, disturbed, or even angry.

To get the real impact of what Jesus was doing we need to get a little bit geeky here. In Jesus' day everyone in Israel spoke in the Aramaic language. The New Testament is written in the Greek language. This means the Gospel writers took what Jesus said in Aramaic and then translated it into Greek. So, when we read the Scripture in Greek, or in an English translation (or some other language) that has been translated from the Greek, we aren't hearing precisely what Jesus' audience would have heard. You have heard that things sometimes get "lost in translation," and that is true. I'm not saying the Bible doesn't accurately present the heart of the message of Jesus, but I am saying sometimes translation means we miss out on nuances that would have been more obvious in the original languages.

But I want to draw your attention to something quite cool: One of the Gospel writers does help us better understand what Jesus' original audience would have heard when Jesus called God "Father." The writer of the Gospel of Mark gives us the word Jesus spoke in

Aramaic—*Abba*—and then he offered the Greek translation of the word, to help the Greek audience to grasp the nuance. Here is the way it reads in your New Testament: "Abba, Father," he said, "everything is possible for you. Take this cup from me. Yet not what I will, but what you will."[26]

Andy quotes someone I will call Jerry (again, more about him at the end of the book.) Jerry is a noted scholar who did a great deal of research, and here's what he came up with.

> To this day nobody has produced one single instance in Palestinian Judaism where God is addressed as "my father" by an individual person, Furthermore, nowhere in the immense literature of ancient Judaism is there a single instance of the invocation of God as Abba. It is a word of utmost intimacy and familiarity. It has the babbling sound that a Jewish infant would use toward his father, the equivalent of Dada. But it is more than that. Grown up sons and daughters call their fathers Abba as well, but only in the context of the greatest tenderness and familiarity. It is never a word used in Jewish prayers because to the Jewish mind it would have been irreverent and therefore unthinkable to call God by this familiar word.[27]

What professor Jerry is telling us here is that with the use of this one word, Jesus did enough to put him in the category of "outrageous." Jesus called God "Abba" and then, as we will see, he taught his disciples to do the same. Jesus was not only saying we can address God as our father, but Jesus was saying we can approach God with the same confidence and intimacy of a child approaching his dad. Jerry published his work about this in 1965. Since then, others have done more research and feel that perhaps he had overstated his case a bit. Other scholars have noted that there was no other word in Aramaic to describe one's father but "Abba," so it was used throughout a person's life. But the main thrust of Jerry's idea still stands. The Jews of Jesus' day were not used to calling God "Father" with the use of *any* word, particularly not one used by toddlers.

Today, because of Jesus and because we live in a culture that has been somewhat Christianized for the past 1700 years, it is no longer a shock to us to hear someone praying to "our Father in heaven." In fact, if you are from a Catholic or Anglican background, you have probably prayed the "Our Father" countless times. But, let me offer another example to help us understand how shocking this would have been in Jesus' day.

Imagine this: you are a teenager in Israel— let's say you are eighteen—and one day you wander up and join a crowd of people listening to a teacher you've never heard of. After the crowd breaks up, you go back home and tell your parents that you heard this man saying a lot about how God loves us and how we can address God in prayer as "Abba." Your father hears this and responds: "What? That's outrageous! How dare he say that? Does he have no respect for our Almighty God, may his great name be blessed? He is trying to corrupt your generation. Do not go out there to hear his teaching again. You are to stay away from that man!" It would not surprise me if there were a number of scenes that played out like that.

But me try another scenario for a twenty-first century crowd: Suppose you go to a funeral or memorial service and at some point, the youngest son of the deceased rises to share, but he first says he would like to pray. After a few awkward moments of silence, the first words out his mouth are "Uh, hey, dude, hey, big dude in heaven, I've got a bone to pick with you." That kind of phrasing would definitely grab our attention and provoke a response. I'm not suggesting you begin addressing God as "Big Dude in Heaven," but I do want to help us understand how Jesus' outrageousness might have been viewed in his day. What he said was shocking. And remember, his bold words got him thrown out of his hometown![28]

However, let's not only focus on how outrageous Jesus' words seemed to be; let's also hear his message for ourselves. His words help us get in touch with what is real and with what matters to God and therefore should matter to us. More on that in the chapters to come.

How He Said We Can Pray

That Jesus so freely and consistently used this name "Abba" for God was controversial enough, but that he taught his followers to do the same made things even worse.

In his famous sermon, the Sermon on the Mount, Jesus talked about prayer in two different sections. In the first section we have what is usually called the Lord's Prayer, and that is the substance of the well-known "Our Father" prayer we mentioned earlier. Jesus essentially said, "Pray like this: 'Our Father who lives in heaven, hallowed be your name,'" and then he went on. His prayer expressed intimacy with the term "Father" or "Abba," but he also communicated reverence in the next phrase, "hallowed be your name."

Earlier in the sermon, Jesus had given his disciples more instructions about prayer: "But when you pray, go into your room, close the door and pray to your Father, who is unseen. Then your Father, who sees what is done in secret, will reward you" (v.6). Jesus was not following the old script, referring to God as simply the father of the nation. Between the use of the word *Abba* and the setting Jesus describes, it's obvious that the person praying would be having a personal audience with God.

Some years after Jesus returned to the Father, one of his followers, whom we know as Paul, wrote that because the Holy Spirit comes to live inside every Christian, we can *all* cry "*Abba*, Father".[29] Again, *Abba* is an Aramaic word, not a Greek word, and Paul was writing letters to places far from where Aramaic was spoken, but apparently the word *Abba* was so unique it had spread its way across cultures. It seems *Abba* had become known among the Christian communities as a special way of addressing God because of the way Jesus had used it.

So, Jesus' followers understood they could have a close, intimate and personal connection with the One whom Andy calls the "Really Real"[30]—the king of heaven and earth. Another author, Tim, made a brilliant observation on this idea: "The only person who dares wake up a king at 3:00 a.m. for a glass of water is a child. We have that kind of access."[31] And this astonishing right of entry into the presence of God is not a minor emphasis in the Gospels. It is the heart of the message. In another letter, Paul made this comment to show that there was no distinction between Jews and Gentiles in Christ: "For through him we both have access to the Father by one Spirit" (Ephesians 2:18). All of Paul's readers—including you and me—needed to understand that each of them could come and wake up the king at three in the morning.

Personal Awe

As I wrote that last paragraph, I had to stop and just sit with it for a while. I have been teaching this powerful truth for at least forty years, but I can't seem to get my mind around it. I am remembering poet Mary's words: "Attention is our endless and proper work." And I am trying to pay attention. Now I am going to break all the rules and give you a long sentence, so hang on. I did not intentionally make it this long but when I wrote it, I just could not seem to stop. I'm going to give it to you in its full unedited form, just the way it came out from me. Here we go: As I give my full focus to this truth (or try to), it still seems outrageous that this human being who grew up as an ordinary "Tommy" in a small town in Alabama and has not been to a tenth of all the places my rocket scientist friend has been to, and who made his lunch today by mixing guacamole, hummus, and mayonnaise all together, can even now, at 77, be in a place, that could be any place, *and be with* the Ground of Being, the Absolute, the Higher Power who is above all Powers, the Source, the Really Real, the God Who Is Greater than the God I try to envision, and *can have access to him,* even at three in the morning (at the same time millions of other people are having the same kind of access to him), and call him "Dad," but that, in fact, is what Jesus is teaching us and me—yes, in the bathroom (which is where I was when I first had this thought). Full stop.

Go ahead read that long sentence again if you need to. I almost want to apologize for getting so personal, but then I'm wanting to share what it's like when the Really Real becomes really real to you. My friend Gordon, who has counseled many people, says the way one views God determines so much of what you will do with your life. What a revolutionary view of God Jesus gave us!

I guess it is obvious that when I try to grasp Jesus' words, I completely stand in awe, and I pray, "My God—Abba, Abba, Daddy, Daddy—help me keep getting this idea deeper and deeper into my heart and never lose it."

I'm hoping you might stop and just sit with this for a while.

Nice People Don't Claim to Be God

Jesus' scandalous way of talking to God and relating to God paved the way for his most outrageous claim: He identified himself as the Messiah who was one with God. Other men had shown up claiming to be the messiah, but Jesus was alone in the way he described his connection with God. If this idea appeared only a few times in the Gospels, we might wonder if some of Jesus' avid followers had just added these things and perhaps jumped to conclusions, but these kinds of statements are embedded throughout the Gospels. Jesus really made these statements—he claimed to be divine. And this is where the outrageousness of Jesus becomes something we all must deal with. This is where it runs right into your wild life—and might even cause it to get wilder.

Many people have called Jesus a great teacher. The Dalai Lama himself recognizes Jesus as either a "fully enlightened being or as a Bodhisattva," which is a very nice compliment. But the famous head of Tibetan Buddhism is not alone in saying nice things about Jesus. I'll name just a few of many: Napoleon, Joan of Arc, Thomas Jefferson, Einstein, Dostoyevsky, Gandhi, Elvis, Bono, MLK, Margaret Thatcher, Denzel Washington and Teddy Roosevelt. (I do wonder if it makes people feel better about themselves to say something nice about Jesus.) However, merely complimenting Jesus may be avoiding the crucial issue, like the elephant in the living room! *Nice normal people don't claim to be God or even insinuate something like that.*

Jesus' outrageous claim, even though made quietly, demands an extreme response. On the one hand, if Jesus was not divine, he was either mentally ill or he was a clever deceiver. On the other end of the spectrum, if Jesus is who he claimed to be, then we must respond appropriately to that truth. Either way, Jesus is not simply a nice moral teacher or a great mystic or a wise sage like Buddha or Mohammed. Of course, I am not the first to say this, but let's unpack the idea some more.[33]

If you remember Jerry from our last chapter, we are going to call on him for a few more remarks. Here is his scholarly comment:

> If we only had two words of Jesus, amen and abba, we would have enough to be able to understand his message. For the word amen indicates that he was one who preached on his own authority, and the word abba indicates that he was one who claimed the most intimate of possible connections with God his Father.[34]

We have already talked about *Abba*, but what is this about the word *amen*? Why does that tell us anything? If you read from an English translation of the Bible, you probably will not realize Jesus used this word at all. But more than eighty times in the four Gospels, usually at the beginning of a sentence, Jesus said, "amen." It usually shows up in an English version as "Truly, I tell you," or "I tell you the truth," or "Truly, I say you." Sometimes Jesus said the word twice, as in, "amen,

amen" which you may have heard translated in older versions as "verily, verily."

We usually say the word *amen* at the end of a statement or prayer to indicate agreement, but when Jesus put it first in his pronouncements, he was stating that he has his own authority to teach. He was claiming an authority that no rabbi would ever claim. Instead of quoting other teachers, he would say, "amen, amen," and sometimes would add, "I say to you." This is why we find this comment at the end of the Sermon on the Mount: "When Jesus had finished saying these things, the crowds were amazed at his teaching, because he taught as one who had authority, and not as their teachers of the law".[35] The word translated "amazed" could be translated "astonished," "surprised," or even "struck with panic." They clearly saw what he was doing, and they had not heard anyone speak with such boldness before. At the very least, Jesus was saying he was a prophet of God. However, when combined with his other statements, we see he was claiming much more. How dare he?

If I were writing a master's thesis, I might list dozens of examples of how Jesus went further, but here I will mention only three.

First, we have Jesus delivering the Sermon on the Mount and saying at the beginning, "I didn't come to destroy the law and the prophets but to fulfill them".[36] Then in the following verses, we hear six times, "You have heard it said... but I say it to you".[37] On his own authority, Jesus declared the old standards were being superseded by new standards of the invading kingdom of God.

If all this weren't enough, at the conclusion of the sermon he stunned his audience with these words:

> "Not everyone who says to me, 'Lord, Lord,' will enter the kingdom of heaven, but only the one who does the will of my Father who is in heaven. Many will say to me on that day, 'Lord, Lord, did we not prophesy in *your* name and in *your* name drive out demons and, in *your* name, perform many miracles?' Then I will tell them plainly, 'I never knew you. Away from me, you evildoers!'" (italics added).[38]

Do you hear what this man said? Not only was he claiming authority to bring a new standard, but he declared that he will one day be in the role of judge. People will be judged on their response to *him*.

Whereas the prophets before Jesus had called people to listen to the voice of God and follow his word, they never exhorted the people to personally follow them. But Jesus came and put being his disciple at the center of this message. Do the following words sound like an enlightened teacher or a self-centered cult leader? "Anyone who loves their father or mother more than me is not worthy of me; anyone who loves their son or daughter more than me is not worthy of me. Whoever does not take up their cross and follow me is not worthy of me. Whoever finds their life will lose it, and whoever loses their life for my sake will find it."[39] Love Jesus more than father and mother? Outrageous! No highly regarded spiritual leader ever made such a claim. No one, that is, except Jesus.

In the well-known story in the Gospels when Peter stepped forward and said "You are the Messiah, the Son of the living God" Jesus affirmed Peter's confession and then added apparently in the same conversation, "Whoever wants to be my disciple must deny themselves and take up their cross and follow me. For whoever wants to save their life will lose it, but whoever loses their life for me will find it"[40] Everyone listening to Jesus knew that you give your life to God, and you lose your life for God, and so it was clear Jesus was making himself one with God. We are to follow him, and lose our lives for him, and in the process truly find our lives. If Jesus was, in fact, what Christians have claimed for years—God incarnate—these statements make perfect sense. But if Jesus' claims were "a bridge too far," they are outrageous and blasphemous.

The Gospel of John has many such statements, like the one where Jesus said to his critics, "Before Abraham was, I am,"[41] identifying himself with the name God gave when he revealed himself to Moses: "I am that I am."[42] It is fashionable for some modern scholars to claim that the lines where Jesus self-identifies with God must have been added later by the early Christians. Because the Gospel of John was written last of the four Gospels, some skeptical scholars claim the early Christians must have changed Jesus' words to make him seem divine and their new religion seem more credible. However, two points undercut these arguments.

First, divine claims do not only appear in John; they also appear in the other Gospels. The four Gospels agree. We have already quoted several of Jesus' divine claims in the Gospel of Matthew.

Second, discoveries in the last century have revealed that the Gospel of John was written much earlier than what many scholars had claimed. Given what we hear Jesus say in the first three Gospels, it is not surprising at all to hear him say, "I am the way and the truth and the life. No one comes to the Father except through me."[43]

Just before I sent this book off to press, I reread this chapter, and I had two thoughts that I want to share with you.

The first is while Jesus undoubtedly saw himself,

in whatever sense you want to think of it, as being God come among us, that was never Jesus' main message. His focus was never on himself. It seems to me that we must honestly deal with his claims, but those were not his emphasis.

The second thing is that while I see a logic in what we have talked about, I realize that for some of you that is not persuasive. You are not moved by logic. You are moved by story, and for you we're going to say more about the outrageous love in the Jesus story in the next chapter. But that will be good for the "logic people" as well.

So, as you ponder your one wild and precious life, who do you think Jesus was? Was he a complete fraud, or simply a very good teacher, or the One with the right and authority to tell you about *Abba*, and then say to you, "*Amen, amen*, come and follow me"? Can you sit with that for a while?

Chapter 9

Even My Enemies?

In 1962, American songwriters Burt Bacharach and Hal David, who later went on to fame, began working on a song. They first offered it to Dionne Warwick, who turned it down, feeling it sounded a little too country for her. Bacharach himself didn't care that much for the song and was reluctant to offer it to other singers, but Jackie DeShannon liked it and recorded it in 1965. The song: "What the World Needs Now Is Love (Sweet Love)." Most of you are humming the lyrics, at least in your mind, right now. The song has been covered by dozens of artists from the likes of, yes, eventually, Dionne Warwick, to the Staples Singers, to Tony Bennett, to the Sesame Street Singers. My favorite may be a virtual edition done by students from Berklee School of Music during the 2020 Pandemic.[44]

The lyrics of the song do not describe Jesus' central message, but you would have to say, they come very close. Scholars agree almost unanimously that Jesus' main theme was that the kingdom of God had arrived and was breaking into our present age. And love? Love was right there as the highest quality in the kingdom. It starts with the insanely generous love of God and flows out from there to all people. Jesus would have agreed that "what the world needs now is love." By that he would not have meant the overly sentimental or saccharine version of the word, but the serious business of respecting that each person is made in the image of God and really caring for each other's needs. And for Jesus, the world will find that kind of love in the kingdom of his Father.

You might be wondering how the outrageousness of Jesus comes through in his teachings on love. Here again, Jesus does not disappoint. Others preached love, but the love Jesus called for went beyond all reasonable bounds. In a word, the kind of love he called for was outrageous.

Giving Aid to Your Enemy?

Israel's history is replete with vile and hated enemies, from the Egyptians and Canaanites to the Philistines, Assyrians, Babylonians, Seleucids, and the Romans. Israel had few friends and many enemies.

One didn't mention love in the same sentence with any of these nations. From passages he quotes, it is obvious that Jesus loved the Psalms found in the Hebrew Scriptures, but Jesus does not take the attitude toward enemies that you find in the Psalms. Those nice songs had some harsh words in them for enemies. No, here comes Jesus, and in the Sermon on the Mount he says:

> "You have heard that it was said, 'Love your neighbor and hate your enemy.' But I tell you, love your enemies and pray for those who persecute you, that you may be children of your Father in heaven. He causes his sun to rise on the evil and the good and sends rain on the righteous and the unrighteous."[45]

In regard to this statement, let me quote a passage I wrote in an earlier book:

> For the first time in the Sermon on the Mount (and in the New Testament, for that matter), we hear Jesus speak the word "love." How interesting that his first command for us to love found in the Gospels is the command to love our enemies. What the people had heard was, "Love your neighbor and hate your enemy." This statement was never made in the Old Testament, but

one can understand why it would have become a common thought. (Again, remember David's words about his enemies in the Psalms.)

Jesus raises the bar as high as it will go in preaching this radical ethic of love: "Love your enemies." Don't hate them; don't be bitter toward them; don't seek revenge; don't hope they will have bad fortune; and don't want to remove them from your sight. No, instead care about them, want them to be blessed, and take action to show goodwill toward them. If we have not realized it already, we certainly see in this command the need for supernatural help to live the kingdom life.[46]

We can well imagine the kinds of responses Jesus might have received to his message: *Love your enemy? What in the world is Jesus talking about? In the first place, why would I want to love the lousy Romans? They invade our land. They take control. They appoint the leaders they want. They require their taxes. They brutally crucify our friends who resist them. Why would I love them? In the second place, how in the world would I do that? Where I am supposed to get the... whatever it would take to do kind things for such nasty people? Where would I even start? This man just keeps saying outrageous things!*

If I had been one of Jesus' advisors, I probably would have suggested that he hold back his message about love for enemies until he had really made a great connection with the people, and then had taught them about loving their own families and loving their friends. I would have suggested first warming up his followers and then gradually breaking them into this more radical teaching. Who knows? Maybe Peter tried that. Maybe the Gospels don't tell us about all the rebukes Peter received.

Jesus had a different approach. A whole new way of thinking was breaking into this world. That's what the kingdom of God was all about. The message of loving people was at the center of it, and that message was that there must be no bounds to this kind of love. (By the way, if you decide at some point you want to take a deep dive into the concept of loving your enemy, I'll give you some direction at the end of the book.)

Love that Breaks Every Barrier

Also, in the previous book I just referred to, I included a simple diagram like this to show how love might look on a continuum:

Loved ones
Friends--Enemies[47]

Of course, we all understand the need to love our

family and close friends, but Jesus is calling for a love that goes all the way across the spectrum. That is going to mean loving a lot of people who aren't close to us but are people we encounter along the way. They don't rise to the level of enemies, but they're not particularly close friends either. Basically, Jesus is calling us to love every person who breathes. He did not just preach this; he lived it. He broke every social barrier and loved people other rabbis often wouldn't go near.

The Outcast Barrier

One day while Jesus was teaching in someone's home, several friends brought a paralyzed man to Jesus. First, Jesus told the man his sins were forgiven, and that statement horrified the religious teachers, who said no one but God can forgive sins. But then Jesus said, "I want you to know that the Son of Man has authority on earth to forgive sins... I tell you, get up, take your mat and go home."[48] And the man did as Jesus instructed. This man was one of many who experienced the healing love of Jesus.

Others included Peter's mother-in-law, the servant of a Roman centurion, a woman with a bleeding disorder, a deaf and mute man, several other men who were blind, a man who had lost his ear due to an impulsive move by Peter, and many more.

Jesus showed loved across the spectrum, and his care and concern went above and beyond. Early on in his ministry, we find Jesus healing a man with leprosy. Lepers were considered as outcasts in their society. Jesus healed the man *by touching him,* which was something absolutely to be avoided. Not only did Jesus bring healing to the man's body, but he gave him the human touch that means so much to our minds and hearts.

The Gender Barrier

In Jesus' culture, rabbis and teachers, and even men in general, did not talk to women in public. But that did not stop Jesus. His revolutionary attitude toward women must not go unnoticed. A woman who had been caught in adultery was brought to Jesus by the teachers of the law, who claimed she should be stoned to death as the law commanded. It was in this setting that Jesus uttered those famous words, "Let any one of you who is without sin be the first to throw a stone at her." He then gave her his assurance that she was forgiven.[49]

Then there was the woman Jesus met at a well in Samaria, who had three strikes against her. First, she was a woman; second, she was a Samaritan; and third, she was a serial divorcée or widow. Undeterred, Jesus broke all the social norms and had a conversation with her, offering her living water. Transformed by the whole experience, the woman returned to her town and persuaded a multitude to come out and meet Jesus.

Another incident with a woman occurred, remarkably, in the home of a Pharisee who had invited Jesus for a meal. At one point something horribly awkward occurred as a woman from the streets crashed the party, coming in with perfume and began to anoint Jesus' feet. This woman was known for living a sinful life, and the host was horrified that Jesus allowed her to continue: *Look, she's kissing his feet!* In one of the most dramatic scenes in the Gospels, Jesus delivered a blistering rebuke to the Pharisee in the man's own house, praised the woman for her love, and pronounced her forgiven.[50]

I mentioned earlier that writing this book itself has been a wild ride. After I had written these thoughts about women, another woman showed up at my door. Well, the woman herself didn't show up, but her book did. In the spirit of keeping things informal, let me call her Carol and quote a few of her words here:

> Jesus' association in public with women who were not his kin was a scandalous breach of decorum and a challenge to the gender boundaries of the first century....
>
> The women Jesus knew were active facilitators and strong, indispensable allies in his mission....
>
> Remarkably, women stood with him through the fierc-

est battle of all, while his male disciples ran for cover....

A view of manhood that insists the top spot belongs to a male, in any context, is difficult to reconcile with Jesus' words. That's how hard it is to be the kind of man who follows Jesus....

His life is a constant rejection of the pillars of patriarchy.[51]

Want to talk about something outrageous? There you have it. Jesus had a care for people that broke through one of the toughest barriers of his day: the gender wall.

The "Enemy" Barrier

Love your enemies? Well, the hated tax collectors could fit into that category. These were men who had cozied up to the Roman government and had agreed to collect taxes from their fellow Jews, often corruptly charging more than they should or keeping more of the money for themselves. What's not to love? Perhaps they weren't strictly enemies, but they were hacks who did the enemy's bidding.

We know Jesus already had one tax collector in his group, and then one day he spotted another tax collector who was short of stature and had climbed a tree so he might see Jesus. Jesus called him down and invited himself to dinner at the man's house. Before the day was over the man's life had been changed and his old attitude toward money discarded. He confessed his sin and mapped out a plan of repentance. We see that he felt loved, perhaps for the first time.[52]

Jesus' example here demonstrates several powerful truths for us: *Your enemy was made in the image of God just as you were.* He or she has all the potential you have of becoming one of God's beloveds. The look on the face of your enemy may seem to betray that idea, but nevertheless, it is true.

Jesus cared about people across the spectrum: from his mother, Mary, to his disciples who walked with him; to outcasts like the man with leprosy and the blind and the deaf; to women in all kinds of distressing situations with no man to speak up for them; and to "enemies" like the Roman centurions and tax collectors. Jesus showed that the central characteristic of his kingdom was love, because that was the central attribute of God the Father. I never thought I would be quoting a tweet in one of my books, but it's a new day, and I have to thank John (you know the drill) for this tweet: "God is shockingly and scandalously inclusive."[53] That is what people learn from Jesus.

Nobody in Israel at the time of Jesus was singing,

"What the world needs now is love, sweet love," but Jesus knew long before songwriters David and Bacharach that love was exactly what the world needed. Just because many who have called themselves Christians have miserably failed to show Jesus' outrageous kind of love to the world does not mean Jesus was wrong. On one occasion Jesus said to the people, "Why do you call me, 'Lord, Lord,' and do not do what I say?"[54] How often have those words described so many who claimed to wear his name?

If the outrageous things Jesus said about himself are true, then the outrageous kind of love he described can still be lived out today, even love for our enemies. In spite of centuries of failure, it can be done—it *is* being done.

Does that kind of love interest you? Would you like to see it? Will you embrace it as part of your plan for your one wild and precious life?

Chapter 10

Jesus, Yes. Church, No.

When you first read the title of this chapter, "Jesus, Yes. Church, No," you may think I'm trying to get your attention, but wonder if with some sleight of hand, I'm going to turn the tables on you. But I actually mean those words in a straightforward and literal sense. Of course, I will explain, but I do encourage you to say yes to Jesus and no to "church." After I explain, you may still feel I have done a bit of a bait and switch on you. But let's see.

This chapter is a bit different in that I'm not so much talking about something outrageous that Jesus said or did, as I am making my own outrageous statement. At least some may see it that way. So let me give you my headline statement right up front: I believe the word *church* should never have appeared in the English

Bible. You might want to read that again and sit with it for a minute. I am convinced that using the word *church* was one of the worst mistakes the translators made, beginning at least in the year 1611, when the King James Version was translated. To be clear, I'm saying that the word *church* should never have been used in connection with Jesus. But you deserve an explanation because almost everybody, when they think of Jesus, thinks of the word church. And most Christians will tell you that if you want to follow Jesus, you will need to be a part of a church or at least you will need to do what we call go to church. So, what in the world am I saying? Am I taking this outrageous thing way too far?

The Greek word that is translated "church" is the word *ecclesia*. Let's take a look at the only two places the word *ecclesia* is attributed to Jesus by a Gospel writer. You'll see that I'm going to print it as the Greek word *ecclesia*, not the English word *church*.

1. Simon Peter answered, "You are the Messiah, the Son of the living God."

   Jesus replied, "Blessed are you, Simon son of Jonah, for this was not revealed to you by flesh and blood, but by my Father in heaven. And I tell you that you are Peter, and on this rock I will build my *ecclesia*, and the gates of Hades will not overcome it."[55]

2. "If they still refuse to listen, tell it to the *ecclesia*, and if they refuse to listen even to the *ecclesia*, treat them as you would a pagan or a tax collector."[56]

In Jesus' day, and this is important, the word *ecclesia* was a common word, not a particularly religious word. It meant an assembly, gathering, or congregation of some kind. Since Jesus spoke aramaic and his words were translated into Greek, we don't really know what word he used. Jewish translators use this word to translate the gathering of God's people as described in the Hebrew scriptures. Most literally it meant "called out." When ancient Athens practiced democracy, the ruling group was known as the *Ekklesia*. It was the large assembly that conducted the business of the city state. In the ancient world there were many *ecclesiae* (plural) for different purposes. The key thing to understand is that the word was all about people who had some particular work or goal. So, in a modern setting, a grand jury would be an excellent example of an *ecclesia*. A Senate committee to investigate an assassination would be an *ecclesia*. A "Blue Ribbon Commission on Homelessness" would be an *ecclesia*. Maybe you could say the Argentine *futbol* (soccer) team or the NFL New England Patriots team is an *ecclesia*.

We can see from the biblical texts from Matthew that Jesus planned to bring his own *ecclesia* into being. His group or assembly or community would be comprised of people who accepted *his* outrageous claims and outrageous statements and who were devoted to carrying out *his* business (of *his* kingdom) in the world. Jesus had every intention of starting something, but it was not a "church." The word *church* is a made-up English word, created for religious purposes. The roots of the word *church* have to do with a physical building. In almost any dictionary the first definition of *church* is a building for religious use. The word does not come close to being a good translation of *ecclesia*.

So how did *church* get to be the main word associated with groups of Christians? It's a fairly complex story, but here are some basic facts: Several English Bibles were translated and produced before the famous King James Version. The majority of them translated the word *ecclesia* as they should have, as assembly, gathering, or congregation. When James I of England decided to sponsor a new translation in 1607, he gave the translators a list of thirteen "suggestions," and one of those was that they use the word "church" to translate *ecclesia*. (But remember he is the king!) Since as king, James I was the head of the Church of England, I can only assume he wanted to remain head of something more official-sounding than a gathering or assembly. This Bible, released in 1611, eventually became known as the King James Version (KJV) or the Authorized Version (AV), and it became so ingrained into the English-speaking culture that virtually every English translation since has used the word *church*, even though most translators know other words are much better. My guess is that most of them felt the burden of hundreds of years of history and decided it just wasn't worth the effort to try and undo a wrong. Sadly, the word *church* takes us far afield from what Jesus really had in mind, and it carries centuries of baggage with it . Today for many people, it's a dark word, associated with various abuses or at least with hierarchy and bureaucracy.

I worked in campus ministry during the latter part of the 1960s. During those years it was not unusual to see some of the marching and protesting students carrying signs that said "Jesus, yes; the Church, no." What they were saying is that while they were inspired by Jesus, they found no use for the institutional church. During those years, I spent quite a lot of time showing student seekers that if you wanted to follow Jesus you also should to be committed to a group of Jesus followers, but I think my job could have been easier without the word *church*.

It occurred to me that those who introduced the

word *church* into our spiritual vocabulary may have meant very well. They may have been trying to create a special word that would designate God's people as distinct from other groups that get together. But if that was their intention, they were trying to do something that Jesus and the writers of the New Testament did not try to do. They may have given us a word, instead, that now carries with it all kinds of darkness and hardly sparks joy in the lives of many who hear it.

Before we go further, let me connect two words for you. One is this word *ecclesia*, and the other is the word *baselia* (*Greek for kingdom*) as in "the kingdom of God." Some people think the *ecclesia*, or in their parlance, the church, is the same thing as the kingdom of God. But when Jesus came, his main message was introducing the kingdom of God—he spoke of it over and over again. As we have seen, he mentioned the *ecclesia* twice. So, what is the difference? I think I can make it simple: the kingdom of God is the reign or rule of God that is breaking into this present age. Jesus' *ecclesia* is the group of people who have bound themselves together in their commitment to live and proclaim the kingdom of God on earth, both with their words and their deeds. The kingdom is much more expansive than the *ecclesia*, but the *ecclesia* finds all of its purpose in the kingdom. The *ecclesia* has the purpose of showing the kingdom to the world in word and in deeds.

Jesus' Community in Action

I don't want to be misleading. If you are drawn to this man Jesus, and you want him to guide your plan for your life, that plan will involve you connecting with other people who are equally serious about Jesus and the kingdom of God. This group's purpose will be to practice all Jesus taught about loving and taking care of each other and helping one other to grow spiritually. They will also share the message of God's insanely generous love with others outside their group. I know one congregation of Jesus followers who refer to themselves as Christ's Healing Community. That name is so much closer to what Jesus had in mind than the word *church*. Jesus' plan is for every person who follows him be part of a healing community where their life flourishes and where they help others' lives to flourish. (By the way, some groups of people who call themselves a church do reflect the kind of loving community Jesus intended. It's just that, in my opinion, the word *church* is not the best way to describe them.)

I don't mean to disparage something that people care very much about. People have literally laid down their lives to help build the kind of *ecclesia* Jesus wanted. They inherited the word *church* and did their best to define it in ways that it would be true to Jesus' vision. I do not want in any way to disrespect them. I am not trying to find villains in the story (Although King James would be a good candidate!), but I'm advocating for an almost impossible change that I think would reorient every assembly, congregation, gathering, or "Jesus team" trying to be loyal to him. I am thankful for all the places where Christ's healing community exists, regardless of what name is on the building or described on a website.

So far, I've been the one making outrageous statements in this chapter, but let's turn back to Jesus and something outrageous he said in regard to this word *ecclesia*. Did you see what he said in that first passage? He said, "On this rock I will build my *ecclesia*, and the gates of Hades will not overcome it." Jesus promises that the forces of death, darkness, and evil will not be able to overcome his group. How can he make such a bold statement? How does he know what the future holds?

At one time I had several meetings with man who taught Greek for many years in Boston. He thought my idea of translating *ecclesia* as "team" is not a bad idea. So, if we think about Jesus' group as a team, Jesus is saying he's going to bring together a team and, in the final analysis, his team will not lose. This community of Jesus followers will not be blotted out. This group will make many mistakes, take some terrible wrong turns, and do some things that are at odds with Jesus' kingdom message. An academic discipline we call "church history" has documented many of those errors and wrongs, but even so, a group of faithful Jesus followers will continue on and will not lose.

After his resurrection, Jesus would tell his disciples that he was going to be with them always, even to the very end of the age. (More on that in the next chapter.) This little group in first-century Palestine was going to start something that would last until the very end of time.

That's a pretty outrageous claim, especially considering it came from a man who had a short ministry, never wrote a book, never traveled outside his own tiny region, and was executed as a criminal. He also said to this little group, "As I have loved you, so you must love one another. By this everyone will know that you are my disciples, if you love one another."[57] Jesus actually thought that his serious followers would be able to demonstrate a kind of love that would make the world take notice. His community would be flawed and have lots of brokenness. Was Jesus just dreaming? Or did he know something we don't?

Jesus gathered a community, but not a perfect one. It would be a community on its own wild ride and one needing a lot of grace and that insanely generous love from God. By the way, I can't just tell you to throw your lot with any group that calls itself a church. Their only problem will not be the use of that word. So many are just interested in keeping traditions, or so it seems, and not really yearning to be the kind of community Jesus was calling for. But I can tell you, that if you are seeking that kind of community and are very open to letting the Spirit of God lead you, I'm pretty sure you'll find it. Jesus said something to that effect, and it can be found.[58]

By the way, don't charge out and paint over the word *church* wherever you see it, at least not yet, and never without permission. Instead, maybe you can join me in trying to find other ways to talk about how Jesus gets people together.

Of course, I cannot end this chapter without asking: Do you plan to get your wild life into his kind of flawed, wild but Jesus-focused community? I hope I didn't mislead you. The man himself said it's part of the plan.

Chapter 11

No Way!

I recently began experimenting with one of the new artificial intelligence (AI) websites. (By the time some of you read this, there is no telling where AI will have taken us.) I asked Mr. or Ms. ChatGPT to tell me how the world would be different if we had never heard of Jesus. It quickly generated seven major changes that would be part of our world if Jesus had never existed or if we had never heard of him. I followed that query up with just a normal Internet search, asking the same question. One of the first results that came up was a long article from a national newspaper detailing how radically different culture and society would be, particularly in the Western World, if Jesus had never been known to us.

Here is an important fact: *if the disciples of Jesus had*

not been fully convinced that he'd been raised from the dead after his brutal crucifixion, we never would have heard of Jesus. It is only because of this *one* event, the resurrection, that the message of Jesus was spread outside the little region where he lived. If that early community (ecclesia) of people, which at one point numbered over five hundred, had not been fully convinced that they had seen the resurrected Jesus, you and I would have never heard of Jesus. He would have been viewed as just another failed messiah, of which there were many, whose names might be found only in an obscure reference in some Ph.D. dissertation.

Many books and articles take a deep dive into the evidence for the resurrection. We will not do that in this book, but I will put some comments at the end with the notes if you want to pursue more study.

Here's another important fact to consider: People don't risk their lives for something they know is a lie. Many early witnesses risked their lives—and some died—because of their claim that they'd seen Jesus risen from the dead. Almost every leader who saw Jesus' resurrection went to his or her death rather than deny it. I recall reading one scholar many years ago who wrote that while his scientific approach would not allow him to go so far as to say Jesus' resurrection was a historical fact, he had to admit that *something happened*.

Something happened to produce the kind of faith we see in those disciples.

Our author friend Andy, who is quite the scholar himself, has some interesting things to say about this. Andy describes the way many thinkers, particularly those who lived 150 to 200 years ago in the heyday of rationalistic thinking, tried to come up with naturalistic explanations for the resurrection, and he says this:

> Another indication of the failure of the naturalistic theories is that each one was disproven by the nineteenth century liberals themselves. These scholars refuted each other's hypotheses, thereby leaving no viable alternative.[59]

In other words, when one thinker would propose a theory that offered a rationalistic explanation for the resurrection, oftentimes before believing Christians even had time to respond, other skeptics would shoot the theory down. All of the skeptics' alternative explanations were refuted by others within their own community. As it turns out, the best way to explain the life-changing faith of the early disciples is to acknowledge that they had seen the resurrected Jesus.

One of my favorite comments about this comes from Andy, who wrote:

> His contemporaries killed him, but he didn't have the good taste to stay dead. He continues to bother us. We evade him, distort him, attempt to turn him into a preacher or a prophet, a political radical or a serene moralizer. But his audacity and his integrity are too strong for our attempts to categorize him. He keeps breaking those bonds as he broke out of the tomb.... Oh yes, indeed it would have been much better for all concerned if Jesus, the self-proclaimed son of God, would go away. But he hasn't, and he won't, and he never will.[60]

Such an appropriate comment: "He did not have the good taste to stay dead." Does that describe Jesus, or what? Jesus was outrageous, astounding, astonishing, always going outside the box. In this case he went outside the tomb, instead of staying in—where any other good upstanding failed messiah would have stayed.

I can well imagine the reaction of some of those who had opposed Jesus. They hear that Jesus' disciples, some forty days after his crucifixion, are out there stirring up the crowds with the story of his resurrection from the dead. I don't know what their Aramaic version of this would have been, but I imagine that some version of "Surely not! No way!" was often heard. Just when they thought they were rid of Jesus, now this.

"Now this" just happened to be the most important

event in human history. If Jesus did, in fact, come out of that tomb and appear body, soul, and spirit, to his disciples over a period of forty days, they had to pay attention; they had to be in awe, and they had to tell someone. And they did. Because of the resurrection, history changed. Because of the resurrection, our lives can also change.

Before his death and resurrection, Jesus had been teaching that the "age to come" (the kingdom of God) was breaking into "the present age." But there was a time when he said this: "Truly [Amen] I tell you, some who are standing here will not taste death before they see the kingdom of God come with power".[61] While there is debate as to when was fulfilled—when those believers saw the kingdom of God—in my view, the resurrection was the time. The resurrection was the supreme moment when the world of the future broke into the present world. What we have here is far more than the resuscitation of a dead body: what we have is the invasion of a whole new order of life.

After the shock of Jesus' death and resurrection, the disciples needed time to process their astonishment, their questions, and their doubts—yes, some doubted at first. Then they became resolute, and you could not stop them from talking about what they had seen and heard.[62] Just as the cross had been the "kingdom come" in that it exemplified generous suffering and insanely generous suffering love, so now the resurrection OF JESUS—again, body, soul and spirit, was the "kingdom come" with power, showing that even death was not supreme or final when it was confronted by the loving outrageousness of Jesus.

Indeed, that is the point often made in the New Testament: that the resurrection is a powerful foretaste of what is to come for those who follow Jesus. Jesus was all about first living the kingdom of God here on earth, but this was just the beginning. Sometimes this idea is called "the now/not yet" paradox. Jesus' followers experience the reality of the kingdom *now*, but there is also a *not yet* element which we look forward to.

Mary Oliver reminded us that we have one precious life. Jesus showed us that that life is so precious that it needs to flourish both now and, in the age to come. Life is precious and valuable because it is meant for much more than what we see around us right now, as amazing as it is. This world *is* our home, we're not just passing through—but we're also made for more. Does your plan for your one wild and precious life involve something more than what we see? Does any other path lead to the resurrection of body, soul, and spirit?

Chapter 12

The Life? Yes, *the* Life.

With this chapter, we come full circle. We started with Mary Oliver asking, "What is it you plan to do with your one wild and precious life?" Now her question runs head on into the answer—the outrageous answer—given by Jesus.

But first let's take another line from Mary Oliver: "Listen—are you breathing just a little and calling it a life?"[63] Although far too many people go through life like this—barely breathing, half-heartedly living—most of us long to find a life that is full, a life that counts.

Your life is valuable, significant, and precious, and it can be full of meaning. But in many cases our lives are empty and there's still too much darkness, but Jesus has the audacity to say, "I've got something to give you that will change you and fill up all the emptiness, and

I've got light that will shine in all your darkness."

There is no shortage of advice out there in our culture about how to find life. Here is just a sampling of what is typical:

- Look Out for #1 (Robert Ringer)
- Be the best version of yourself.
- "Think and Grow Rich" (Napoleon Hill)
- Believe in yourself.
- Be all you can be. (courtesy of the US Army).
- Practice self-care and self-compassion (an oxymoron?)
- Be your authentic self.
- Know yourself.
- "The privilege of a lifetime is to become who you truly are." (Carl Jung)

What all these statements, and others like them, have in common is the idea that you find life by reaching out and taking hold of it yourself. You will notice that *you* take center stage in all of these statements with a focus on *self*. For most people this seems to make very good sense.

Before we look at Jesus' very different answer, let's ask if he's really a reliable source, relevant to our day and time. Many college students asked me this question back in the 1960s, 1970s. and 1980s. Andy says he got this question a lot too. The answer he gave then still applies today: "If God really was present in Jesus in a unique way, if we are really privileged to be in intimate contact with the Really Real on a basis of affectionate familiarity, then this good news is overwhelmingly relevant."

In other words, if Jesus was the Messiah of God, leading the invasion of the kingdom of God into this world, he will always be relevant. Relevant then, relevant now, relevant in the year 3024, if the world survives the threat of nuclear war and climate change. Relevant, yes. Popular, no. Those are two different things.

Lose Your Life to Save It

By now, you won't be surprised that given his outrageousness, Jesus gives quite a different solution to the question of finding life. While everyone else is trying to find their authentic self or grab all the gusto they can get, Jesus says, *lose it.* Yes, lose it. Lose your life! Give it up! Surrender it! He even goes so far as to say, put it on a cross. Yes, crucify it. Let it die. Now that might sound a little bit like Eastern spirituality, where you hear expressions like, "By letting go, it all gets done." But Jesus spoils the syncretism party by saying: "Whoever finds their life will lose it, and whoever loses their life for *my sake* will find it."[64] Did you catch that? "For my sake." Another translation renders it this way: "If you cling to your life, you will lose it; but if you give up your life for me, you will find it." Jesus is not just giving a paradoxical, enigmatic principle of philosophy that you must lose your life in order to find it. No, he is going further and saying you must do more than just lose it in the abstract, but you must lose it *for his sake*: for him, for his purposes, for his vision, for his mission, for his kingdom, because he's convinced that's where you find the Really Real.

Wow! Who does Jesus think he is? Here I have my one precious life, and I'm given the freedom to choose what I'm going to do with it, and he says to lose it all *for him*? Well, we've already established who he thinks he is. We've also established that he is bringing a message that the God of the universe, the Source, the Really Real, has an insanely generous love for us and wants nothing but to give us an abundant life, a flourishing life, a full life, a life full of light. And he is just telling us the truth about how that life can be found.

Now you can easily see why Jesus' message has never been popular. People would much rather hear:

- Keep pursuing all of your ideas, but work in a little room for God somewhere around the edges.

- Keep finding your authentic self, but don't be a totally ungrateful jerk, and from time-to-time tip your hat to the Creator who put you in a pretty amazing world.
- Post nice little sayings on social media about not letting others control your life, and once in a while, include a saying that mentions the divine.
- Keep pursuing all of your material goals, but nurture your spiritual side by reading and writing poetry.

The truth is we would rather hear almost anything other than a call to commit ourselves to something all-consuming. That kind of extremism is dangerous... unless it is an all-out effort to give yourself fully to the most unique human being in history who is full of the divine, insanely generous love of Abba. In that case, it might mean finding life that is rich and flourishing, a life where it feels like your cup is really overflowing, even when suffering. It might mean finding a freedom that goes beyond all of your earlier concepts of freedom and opens you up to receive all kinds of gifts God wants to give. And it might very well mean having a real experience of the presence of God in your life, one you can feel.

It may be that the real meaning of "deny yourself" is to simply start living with deep humility. On the one hand, Jesus says one must deny himself or herself in order to follow him. Just a little bit later he says that unless you humble yourself like a little child you will never enter the kingdom of God. I think he's essentially talking about the same thing. It is about learning to say, "not my will but yours be done," and trusting in the outrageous love of a God who knows more than you do.

Q & A

Let me stop here for a moment. I've been doing a lot of writing (or talking, if you will). Let me stop allow you to ask some questions you may have. Let's have a little hypothetical conversation. This may seem a bit contrived (I guess, because it is), but let me try to imagine some of your questions or comments.

You: Tom, are you saying that once we turn everything over to Jesus, life is just going to be wonderful all the time?

Me: I'm glad you asked that, because if you mean are you going to be able to live without any troubles or difficulties, Jesus was very clear on this point. 'In this world," he said, "You will have trouble.." But then he added, "Take heart. (or be of good cheer). I have overcome the world."[65] Those statements are in the context of him just saying, "My peace I give to you." So, he is promising that, on the one hand those who follow him will still go through the normal challenges of human life. In other places he makes it clear that deciding to follow him may bring more problems than usual because of the opposition they will receive. But on the other hand, he is promising that even in the midst of those challenges one will find a peace from God and the consciousness that the Father in heaven is still embracing them and supporting them. I have been seeking to follow Jesus for 57 years and I can assure you that I have seen some challenging times. I didn't expect it to be otherwise. Jesus never sugarcoated his message. I realized that early on. But at the same time, he has not failed to deliver on his promises. He helps us to hold both pain and joy at the same time.

You: I've read his Sermon on the Mount, and those teachings are hard. I've read that certain people have worn themselves out trying to follow these rules. Doesn't this just add more burden to people's lives?

Me: Perhaps you missed the opening part of that message. Let me take you there and see if you might have overlooked it or not understood it: "Blessed are the poor in spirit for theirs is the kingdom of God."[66] The very first point of the Sermon on the Mount is that we must all be aware of our poverty of spirit and openly acknowledge that. We do not have what it takes to live the life God calls us to, and the very first step to live it is to admit how great our need is. In so many ways Jesus teaches that such humility and honesty about ourselves unleashes the powers of the age to come into our lives enabling us to be much more than we could ever be on our own. Yes, if you try to live the Sermon on the Mount on your own power, it will do more than wear you out. It might even drive you mad. Beyond that, i'm convinced that the sermon is not a list of dos and don'ts. It is the description of a life you can live when you allow the age-to-come to flood into you even in this present world. It is a new vision about how to be human.

You: But I know Christians who seem to be serious about following Jesus and nevertheless they go through serious bouts of depression. When you say Jesus can bring a full life, do you think that promise applies to people who deal with mental illnesses or disorders?

Me: I am not a mental health expert, but I can speak to this as a person who has experienced what you're talking about. I have known the darkness of depression, and not just for a few weeks. The research tells us that about twenty percent of Americans experience some form of mental illness. I'm convinced from experience that Jesus' message does not leave out all those people.

You've heard about autism, which now goes by the

name autism spectrum disorder. Well, I wonder if a lot of disorders are on a spectrum. I've always thought that I was probably on the bipolar spectrum somewhere (although my psychiatrist friend doubts that's possible). And then there are days I think I'm on the OCD spectrum. And then throw in a little bit of anxiety disorder spectrum. And I've already mentioned that I've faced the challenge of depression. I have concluded that all of this lands me somewhere on the *human* spectrum. I'm convinced that what we call mental illnesses is a part of life. One day we may have a totally different term for all these challenges. All lives are going to have difficulties, and struggles with depression or mental illness are going to play a more significant part of some people's lives, but I've seen how the fresh perspective of the kingdom of God helps everyone. It has certainly helped me.

You: I would like you to talk some more about how life in Jesus is wild. I know some Christians who seem to live harried and frenetic lives. They seem to be struggling to keep up with their family and work responsibilities and also do all these things that are involved in the mission of Jesus. Their lives look wild, but not the kind of wild I'm interested in.

Me: Thanks for that question which I think is an incredibly relevant one. You may have heard some of the statistics about how many people are leaving churches these days and are declaring themselves to be part of the "nones"—those with no religious affiliation. I suspect a lot of those people have left because they live pretty harried lives already, and if they don't have deep convictions, it is just easier to leave out the religious part. But there are those who try it, and sometimes their lives just get more and more frenetic. I would say, at times I've been there. If we find that we're living a life that is full of stress without peace and without joy, we might be doing a lot of things in the name of Jesus, but, no, that's not the kind of wild I am talking about.

What I am trying to describe is more like an adventure. You've decided to follow someone you trust, but you don't really know where it's going; you just know that you're going keep taking the next steps of faith, eager to see what's around the next turn. It will bring you some amazing experiences and the development of some pretty incredible friendships. If you look up the word *adventure,* you'll probably find that it usually involves something a bit hazardous. Jesus will definitely get you into that zone because he's not looking for those who just want to stay safe. There will be some challenging lows and times of going through dark valleys, but there will be some incredible heights in which you will learn what it means to truly experience the living God, the loving Abba, Father, the powerful Spirit, the Really Real.

You: As an American, I've heard all my life about the pursuit of happiness. I just heard a report on television, and surveys have determined for the sixth year in a row that Finland is the happiest country on earth. From what I've heard, the Finns are no longer particularly religious. Iceland was number two, and I know they are not all that religious either. If you ask me, religion seems pretty grim. Talking about denying yourself and taking up a cross sounds pretty gloomy. So where does happiness fit in to what you're saying? So, part A of my question is: Can I expect Jesus to bring me happiness? And then there is a B part: did Jesus ever laugh?

Me: Maybe it is a matter of semantics, but I think Jesus wanted something much deeper for those who followed him. What he did talk about was joy, and he said he was giving it to his disciples. Toward the end of his life, he spoke these words: "I have told you this so that my joy may be in you, and that your joy may be complete."[67] They must have believed him and gone on to experience it We find this statement after his resurrection: "Then they worshiped him and returned to Jerusalem with great joy."[68] Joy is talked about in twenty-two of the twenty-seven books of the New Testament, and something like it is referred to in most all of them. It's obvious that followers of Jesus did not find their life in him to be grim and gloomy. Instead, it seems to be a *joyful adventure but, yes, sometimes in the midst of harrowing moments.* That is much more like what I have found.

Now to part B of your question, some have noticed that while the Gospels talk about Jesus weeping, they don't mention him laughing. He did tell some pretty funny stories—they must have brought smiles, if not outright laughter. But here is my take on this topic: laughter plays a huge role in a full life. It's impossible for me to imagine a full, flourishing life without laughter. So, my view is that Jesus not only laughed but he probably laughed a lot.

My wife was a serious follower of Jesus, but she laughed a lot. One of my daughters made up a little book for one of Sheila's birthdays, and the title was: *She Laughed, She Laughed, and then She Laughed Some More.* I still have in my apartment the plaque that was in her office for many years. It simply reads, *Laugh.* I'm looking at it even as I write this. And following her example, I laugh quite a lot these days. Research shows that laughter has so many good outcomes. It reduces stress, boosts immunity, lowers blood pressure, improves mood, and even reduces pain. It also strengthens social bonds. All of those sound like things Jesus would have been for! I'm thankful that the recent television series *The Chosen* shows Jesus laughing and dancing. I think they get it right.

Can I bring Mary Oliver back into our discussion? She wrote:

> "If you suddenly and unexpectedly feel joy,
> don't hesitate. Give in to it.
> ...whatever it is, don't be afraid
> of its plenty. Joy is not made to be a
> crumb."[69]

I think I can hear Jesus saying, "Amen."

You: I assume that even when we try to live for Jesus, we will still make mistakes and have our own sins. How do you keep those problems from ruining this life you're talking about?

Me: That is a struggle the followers of Jesus face every day. I did write another book called *God's Perfect Plan for Imperfect People.*[70] When we commit ourselves to following Jesus, we still remain human beings filled with mixed motives and confusing emotions, facing a massive number of distractions and other challenges. For example, I'm answering your question after getting very little sleep last night. I know this will be one of those days when I'm much more prone to doing the wrong thing. That's why the Scriptures talk about confession and forgiveness and grace. I'm guessing this is also why Jesus talked a great deal about where your heart is. The

God Jesus speaks of is not so much concerned about how perfectly you do something, but where your heart is. A person may miss the mark (which is what the word *sin* really means) and still have a heart that wants to get it right, and that is what this God of outrageous love is most concerned about.

**

Okay, I'm sure I've answered all the questions you'll ever have. LOL. (That's me laughing out loud, for the five or six of you who don't use the Internet.) I imagine you have more questions, but we'll stop there.

Jesus offers the truth that leads to life. Lose your life—your old life that is all tied up with worldly thinking about how to protect yourself and end up on top. Lose your life of competing with God and find the freedom to reflect the image of God that you were created to show to the world. Lose your life of having it your way, and find the life in which you so experience the presence of God that you don't mind losing your life at all.

Shall we ask it one more time: What is it you plan to do with your one wild and precious life? Do you have a better plan than Jesus has? Don't you suspect he's rooting for you to make a good choice, and then keep making it?

Chapter 13

Captivated

We are approaching the end of this little book. What are your thoughts? When you think about your plan for your life in light of Jesus' calling, what are you thinking? Are you seeing some connection? Do you find Jesus irrelevant or interesting or fascinating or frightening? Are you amused? Intrigued? Curious to know more? Are you captivated?

Captivate. There is an interesting word. that means "to influence and dominate by some special charm, art, or trait and with an irresistible appeal."[71] We might use the word in sentences like, "We were captivated by her beauty," or "The scenery captivated our attention" or " His breathtaking ability was absolutely captivating."

"When I wore a younger man's clothes," (thank

you, Billy Joel) and I read the Gospels and books by Andy, and other authors named Dietrich and Clive, I found myself increasingly captivated by Jesus. I've lived a lot of life since then. I've been to mountaintops, and I've been through some dark valleys, literally, but more importantly emotionally and spiritually. I have learned a lot. I know a lot more now about science and the universe. I have even learned some laws of physics. I have learned some things about stocks and bonds and how the economy works. I know a lot more about other world religions and philosophies. But I am still captivated by Jesus. When I write a book like this one, I'm attracted and absorbed all the more.

Is it still possible to be powerfully drawn by a man who lived two thousand years ago, who didn't make it to 35, whose story has been told, and often distorted, in millions of iterations? It may not seem likely, but whenever people closely examine this man Jesus, it is not unusual for them to come away deeply attracted to his blend of gentleness and boldness, his outrageous claims and unselfish servitude, his common touch and commanding presence, his strength of resolve but outrageous love, his torturous death and stunning resurrection. To say it again, he was unconventional, perplexing, unorthodox, extraordinary, unique, bewildering, remarkable—all things you might expect if God was to show up and walk among men.

Even so, with such a vast world filled with people offering ideas for how to live, do you still wonder if it is strange, or even foolish, to base your entire life on one man? I think that's a good question. But let me ask you to think about this. Presently, cosmologists still hope to find life out there somewhere but mostly agree that our planet, the pale blue dot, is very likely completely unique among all the vast universe. Their best estimate is that there are trillions of heavenly bodies in the universe but we might be the only one that experiences a literal riot of life.

Stop for just a few seconds.

Think about that.

Pay attention.

Is that amazing?

But we have the physical evidence that it's very likely true. As "my skeptical friend," nevertheless, said, "It's a miracle that we're even here at all." Given that amazing fact, does it seem so impossible to believe that there might have been one man out of all who've lived on Earth, who was not only the most important person to ever live, but completely unique? If we can believe in a miraculous planet, can we not also believe in the miraculous, outrageous man and the insanely generous love of God he spoke of? And if such a man existed, wouldn't it be quite fitting to be captivated by him?

Some of you might hear this and think that I am hoping to get you interested in Christianity, whatever that is, and could be a lot of different things. No, that is not my interest at all. I actually have never cared for the word Christianity. Let me share with you my goal by telling you about something written by an early follower of Jesus. We don't know if it was a letter or a sermon. We don't know who wrote it, since it was anonymous, and males and a female have been suggested. However, what we do know is the writer had a laser focus, and toward the end exhorted the readers "to fix their eyes on Jesus."[72] Now that absolutely describes my goal. Whoever he or she was, that writer knew something about being captivated. When you fix your eyes on Jesus and you keep that focus, it leads to some very good outcomes.

You and I have wild and precious lives, and we just have one. Are you going to spend your one life on some experience that ends up nowhere? Or will you consider spending it on a person who was outrageous—outrageous in all the right ways? Whatever you decide, you're likely going to have a wild ride. Why not take it with someone like Jesus?

Maybe it starts with just being intrigued by Jesus. That's where it seemed to start with those who met him in person. Maybe you're not captivated at this point, but you're intrigued. There's something about this man that's different. Different from other people, different from Jewish teachers, different from Greek philosophers, certainly different from the politicians. What do you really think about *him*? Not what do you think about church scandals or Christian hypocrisy or misguided efforts to combine "church" and state. But what do you think about *him*? Hasn't he done enough or said enough to call for a verdict?

Peter was captivated by Jesus. But he was still on his own journey, and when push came to shove Peter got shoved right off the back of the boat. He shipwrecked his discipleship. Three times he denied he even knew Jesus. But he was still hanging in there. And when he saw that this Jesus, who had said and done so many outrageous things, really came back from the from the dead in the flesh, and not as a ghost, finally Peter's heart was captured for good. And I suppose that a little conversation about love after breakfast one day helped seal the deal.[73]

Where are you on your journey? Have you heard enough about Jesus now to be intrigued? Are you thinking you might hang around long enough to be captivated?

When it comes to Jesus, I know we have barely dipped our toes into deep waters. But I hope I've given you enough to at least begin an adventure or to get back on the road. Actually, by reading this far, you've already taken quite a few steps down the path. You have already come far enough to make a decision that will change the rest of your life. You can make that decision. Or not. *His insanely generous love will never pressure you to do it*, but he won't stop waiting on the front porch to see if you're coming, or to wonder if this might be the night you wake him up at three in the morning.

I am not sure of the nature of Mary Oliver's faith, but she wrote the following, and I want to give her a final word:

I want

to see Jesus,

maybe in the clouds

or on the shore,

just walking,

beautiful man

and clearly

someone else

besides.[74]

Yes, Mary, someone else besides. Someone amazing. Someone captivating.

What is it you plan to do with your one wild and precious life?

Jesus knows a lot about your precious life and he says, "Follow me." If you decide to do that, I suspect that during your journey, you will be in awe. And very likely, you will tell someone.

**

Thank you for reading or listening. At any point on your journey, if you would like to be in touch, you can reach me at my website: tomajones.com. Just look for the button that says, "Contact Tom."

Postscript to All Who Once "Decided"

just want to add a final word to those of you who decided quite some time ago to connect your one life to Jesus.

Some of you are in what I will call the "Amen" group. You remember well when you decided to follow him. It has probably been a wild ride. Your life with him has not been one moment of bliss after another. Just as he promised, in this world you have found troubles. You have learned that he calls us to follow him in suffering. However, you have found him faithful and because of him you have found something rich, something to be compared to a great treasure. You have grown tired at times, but you have found new strength to continue. Not all of your relationships have been wonderful, but you have found common bonds in Jesus that have far surpassed others that you've known. You might relate to these words, written by a first century disciple: "We are hard pressed on every side, but not crushed; perplexed, but not in despair; persecuted, but not abandoned; struck down, but not destroyed."[75] Your faith may have been battered and bruised, but you are thankful for the power of your faith. To say it more correctly, you are so thankful for *him*—the object of your faith. You are still captivated. He is living water, and you have more you want to drink. To read what we've said about him, and you say, Amen! (At age 77, I'm with you in this group, still learning how much more there is to drink.)

But there are others of you who, surprisingly, decided to read this book. Surprisingly, because the glare of an imperfect "church" long ago replaced a clear gaze of the remarkable Jesus. You aren't so captivated by him now as you are consumed by a series of painful experiences. Maybe you're hanging on to your Christian community, but just barely, and without joy. Maybe you've already left and closed the door behind you. Maybe you would give your experiences a D rating. D for "disappointing." Maybe even D for "damaging." It is absolutely possible to be in a group that claims to follow Jesus and find abusive behavior. It happens. I have seen it, and if it happened to you, I'm very sorry. The Jesus I have written about did not approve it. He himself was the victim of such religious behavior and worse. We have strong evidence that he understands why it's difficult for you to see him, but he has not stopped trying to show you who he is. Just maybe, this book is a part of that effort.

I hope you're open to that.

Often two things that are in tension with each other are both true. Some examples:

- Following Jesus can bring you both into connection with encouraging people *and* difficult people.
- The ecclesia can be incredibly valuable and even essential to our own spiritual life *and* be in need of transformation and perhaps even repentance.
- A Jesus group is quite imperfect *and* yet loved by him and used by him despite its imperfections.

In a story you no doubt are familiar with, Peter became the second person to ever walk on water, and he did it when his gaze was fixed on Jesus. However, after a few miraculous steps, he famously turned his focus to the waves and the winds and then sank. When we take our eyes off of him, then the difficult people, the need for repentance and the imperfections of the group will consume our vision and our emotions and eventually our will, and our faith will take a dive. I could encourage you to be more patient or to be more forgiving or more resilient, but I have a feeling that none of that would matter, *if you're not captivated by Jesus.* Perhaps you have heard someone talk about having deep roots for your faith. That is a needed message, but we need a taproot that goes straight down directly into Jesus,

I'd like to say a final word to another group. If you're in this number, I hope you're still listening. Jesus talks about you in one of his most famous stories: "The seed falling among the thorns refers to someone who hears the word, but the worries of this life and the deceitfulness of wealth choke the word, making it unfruitful." At one time you were with him and then you left. You walked away not because "the church" deserved a failing grade. You just went after something else. At some point you were impressed enough with Jesus, that you decided to make him the Lord of your life and you were immersed to share in his death and resurrection. But... (and how big a word that is) ... *But* you started being impressed with other things and you forgot what you had in Jesus.

Jesus' parables pack a powerful punch and point in important directions, but analogies and metaphors and even parables usually break down somewhere. In the parable, those in this group apparently just stayed there. But if you're there, you don't have to stay there. That is how gracious and kind and forgiving Jesus is. He still wants you. He won't for a minute lower the standards for you, but you can still be captivated by him. If you come back and some critic reminds of your past, you'll be able to tell them with a smile, that Jesus dropped all the charges. Plus, he's throwing a party in your honor.

Inspired by Jesus' greatest story, Rembrandt, the great Dutch master, painted "The Return of the Prodigal Son." It depicts the young man on his knees leaning his head against the father's chest as he is embraced by his father. Henry, who is mentioned earlier in this book, spent years contemplating that painting and wrote an entire book about his experience. At one point Henry writes, "I have to kneel before the Father, put my ear against his chest and listen, without interruption to the heartbeat of God."[76] There are so many reasons that I want that more than ever. But beyond that, I want that for you as well, so together we can be in awe.

Some who decided for Jesus are very thankful and want to know more of him. Some are disappointed, but not usually in him. Some have been damaged, definitely not by him. And some have been diverted because of themselves, not because of him. But he is lovingly outrageous. He is outrageously loving. Whatever your story, he can inhabit, enable and energize your one wild and precious life.

Yes, he was a "beautiful man and someone else besides."

**

Characters in Order of Their Appearance:

Mary Oliver: She appears as herself and has helped me be in awe of my wild and precious life, and may have even converted me to poetry.

Andy: Andy is Andrew Greeley. He was a professor of sociology, a journalist, a popular novelist, and a priest. Fifty years ago I bought a small volume that he wrote and on the cover is printed the price of $1.25. Turns out it was money well spent. In fact, I'm hoping my little book will have something of the same impact on you that his book had on me. Having survived more than fifteen moves, this thin paperback is still with me. Not long ago, I picked it back up and reread all 198 pages of small print for the first time in five decades. I tell you this to say, not only do I owe a debt to Mary Oliver for her poetry, but I also owe a debt to Andrew Greeley, who played a key role in inspiring this book. When I first read his work, I thought that it had a misleading title. It's called *The Jesus Myth* (Image Books, New York, 1973). With that title, I am a little surprised I ever bought it.

Early on, Greeley explains what he means by myth, and he is clear that in his view, Jesus is no legend or folktale but one who brings us to the Really Real.

Phil: I quote him in Chapters 7 and 11; he is the well-known writer, Phillip Yancey. I am quoting from his book *The Jesus I Never Knew*.

Henry: This is Henri Nouwen, also a priest, who served as a professor at Notre Dame, Harvard and Yale. He spent ten years of his life serving the disabled in a community in Toronto. His spiritual writings have had impact on many. He makes a brief but spectacular appearance in Chapter 7, and then again in the post script.

Carol: The woman who "showed up at my door" in time to make it into Chapter 7 is Carolyn Custis James. Her book is **Malestrom: How Jesus Dismantles Patriarchy and Redefines Manhood.**

Jerry: This serious guy is Professor Joachim Jeremias. He was a German theologian and scholar of Near Eastern Studies and professor for New Testament studies. He died in 1979. This is probably the first time he's ever been called Jerry. Quotes from him are in Chapter 8.

Tim: This is Timothy Keller who was the founding pastor of Redeemer Presbyterian Church in New York City and the author of many bestselling books. He died quite unexpectedly in 2023. He is also quoted in Chapter 8.

John: He is John Ortburg a bestselling author, and his short but powerful "tweet" made it into Chapter 9.

Dietrich: He is Dietrich Bonhoeffer, the well-known German Lutheran pastor and writer who was executed in a Nazi concentration camp. He makes a brief appearance in chapter 13.

Clive: He, of course, is Clive Staples Lewis, more commonly known as C.S. Lewis, whose conversion from atheism to Jesus led to the writing of many books, including the series known as *The Chronicles of Narnia*. He also is also mentioned in chapter 13.

For Further Study

- For a more comprehensive look at the person of Jesus you might consider my earlier book *No One Like Him*, still in print and available from ipibooks.com.

- For a much deeper dive into the topic of loving your enemies, let me suggest this website: "Following the Prince of Peace in a Culture of Violence" https://www.jesuspeacecollective.com/.

- For a more thorough study of evidence for the resurrection of Jesus, let me suggest "Jesus Online: Did Jesus arise from the dead." https://jesusonline.com/lp/jesus-rise-dead-dp-sch

More about Jesus and "Church"

Did Jesus want a church, like some of these? Or did he want an *ecclesia* made up of people in genuine community? Do most of these things below have little or nothing to do with his vision? Can the "church" be "saved" or do we need to speak of something else? What would a lovingly outrageous Jesus say?

1. I'm going to church today.
2. Was church boring?
3. What are you doing after church today?
4. Since moving to town, we have been church shopping.
5. I'm happy in my church tradition.
6. How is that church different from other churches?
7. How many people are on the church staff?
8. Is church discipline practiced in your church?
9. Your tour will include great churches and cathedrals
10. Among the most famous churches in Europe are Notre Dame in Paris, Saint Peter's Basilica in Vatican City, and Saint Basil's Church in Moscow.
11. Must see churches in America include Saint Pat-

rick's Cathedral, New York City, and Washington National Cathedral, Washington, D.C.

12. She wrote, "The most dangerous place for a woman today is often the church."
13. Church-sponsored schools are accused of scandalous behavior among Native Americans.
14. Do you sing in the church choir?
15. Do you prefer high church or low church?
16. The Memorial Church features a copper dome imported from Italy.
17. What do you think about the separation of church and state?
18. Where is your church located?
19. Is that the church on the corner of 5th and Pine?
20. I forgot and left my coat in the church last Sunday.
21. How many campuses does that church have in the greater metropolitan area?
22. Is that the giant megachurch that you see just as you get off the Interstate?
23. The church lost its steeple in the storm last night.
24. Did your little girls wear their church dresses on Sunday?

25. Church opposition led to rezoning the property.
26. When you were in Jerusalem did you go to the Church of the Holy Sepulcher?
27. Did you go through the humility door of the Church of the Nativity in Bethlehem?
28. How badly was the church's reputation harmed by the Crusades?
29. He wrote, "The church has not yet dealt with its relationship with the Nazi SS."
30. Church-related dating sites.
31. An Open Letter to the American Church.
32. How many children do you pick up with the church bus?
33. Do you feel out of place when you're in church?
34. I have just never had a very good experience with church.
35. I like Jesus, but I'm not much on church.
36. "The Presbyterian Church in America (PCA) and the Presbyterian Church in the United States (PCUSA) differ in several ways."
37. I go to church for the quiet.
38. My church is being out in nature.

39. My church is the Big House in Ann Arbor.
40. How can I get food from the church pantry?
41. Is the Church of Scientology a Christian group?
42. Welcome to the official website of the Church of Satan, founded 1966.
43. The church was involved in the Transatlantic Slave Trade.
44. The former Fourth Church of Christ, Scientist is a historic Christian Science church in San Francisco.
45. The pastor is rethinking the way we do church.
46. The catechism of the Catholic Church
47. The United House of Prayer for All People of the Church On The Rock of the Apostolic Faith
48. Church literature always sells well after he speaks.
49. "White Savior: Racism in The American Church."
50. Having church on Saturday night, frees up our Sundays.
51. I get a creepy feeling when I go in that church.
52. The Restored Church of God – rcg.org
53. She wrote: "The parish church in Bawburgh, near Norwich, was also a pilgrimage church"

54. He wrote, "All wings of the American church have been scandalized by the sexual behavior of leaders."
55. Is the Protestant church exempt from that issue?
56. Church-related colleges and retirement homes.
57. There are disturbing stories in church history.
58. A church is automatically considered tax exempt without filing for 501(c)(3) status.
59. The Woke Church is: (A) the hope of America or (B) a great threat to America?
60. The Ryman Auditorium is the mother church of country music.

Can you add to the list?

Can "church" be "saved?"

What is an honest seeker to think?

Is this a good time to apply the rule of not throwing the baby out with the bathwater?

What would Jesus say?

Do you have a comment?

Notes

1. "Quirky," *Merriam-Webster Dictionary,* https://www.merriam-webster.com/dictionary /quirky#synonyms (accessed July 10, 2024).

2. Mary Oliver, "The Summer Day." *House of Light.* Boston, Beacon Press Reprinted by the permission of The Charlotte Sheedy Literary Agency as agent for the author. Copyright © 1990, 2006, 2008, 2017 by Mary Oliver with permission of Bill Reichblum.

3. "Cosmetic surgery in South Korea." *Wikipedia,* Wikimedia Foundation, .https://en.wikipedia.org/w/index.php?title=Cosmetic_surgery_in_South_Korea&oldid=1157889643 (accessed August 31, 2023).

4. John Eldridge. *Wild at Heart.* Thomas Nelson Publishers, 2001.

5. "Wild," *Dictionary.com.* https://www.dictionary.com/browse/wild (accessed July 10,2024)

6. "Wild," *Merriam-Webster Dictionary,* https://www.merriam-webster.com/dictionary/wild (accessed July 10, 2024).

7. "This World Is Not My Home," song by A.P. Carter, 1931.

8. "The Chance Events that Led to Human Existence," *BBC Online*, https://www.bbc.co.uk/teach/the-chance-events-that-led-to-human-existence/zdjd382, (accessed May 30, 2023).

9. Fabiana Fondevila, "Mary Oliver: poet of awe." *Daily Good,* March 24, 2019, https://www.dailygood.org/story/2246/mary-oliver-poet-of-awe-fabiana-fondevila/(accessed June 1, 2023).

10. Quoted on The Poetry Foundation, https://www.poetryfoundation.org/harriet-books/2019/05/attention-as-a-form-of-devotion-to-mary-oliver (accessed August 31,2023).

11. Quoted from *Long Life,* Essays and Other Writings (Lebanon, Indiana: De Capo Press, 2004).

12. Josh Terry, "This Is Why We Love Outrageous Stories like 'Tiger King,'"*Tudum*, November 2, 2021, (accessed June 1, 2023).

13. "Outrageous." Dictionary.com. https://www.dictionary.com/browse/outrageous

14. "Letter from Thomas Jefferson to John Adams," Encyclopedia Virginia (October 12, 1813). https://encyclopediavirginia.org/entries/letter-from-thomas-jefferson-to-john-adams-october-12-1813/. (accessed March, 2023).

15. Andrew M. Greeley, *The Jesus Myth* (Garden City NJ: Image books, 1973) 69 and 113. In my opinion the title is misleading, since it contains many helpful insights into the life of Jesus and an affirmation of his historical reality.

16. John 8:33

17. Luke 18:19

18. Luke 11:13

19. Greely, 69.

20. Greely, 49.

21. Greely, 49.

22. Henri Nouwen, *The Return of the Prodigal Son: A Story of Homecoming* (New York: Doubleday, 1994).

23. John 3:16

24. See Luke 14:16-23

25. Greely, 92.

26. Mark 14:36

27. Greely, 89.

28. See Luke 4:14-30

29. See Romans 8:15 and Galatians 4:6

30. Greely, 175.

31. Timothy Keller, Facebook post, December 3, 2019.

32. Mary Oliver, "Yes! No!" Famous Poets and Poems .com http://famouspoetsandpoems.com/poets/mary_oliver/poems/15818 (*accessed September 16, 2024*).

33. I am pretty sure it was C.S. Lewis who first helped me see this.

34. Greely, 86.

35. Matthew 7:28-29

36. Matthew 5:17

37. Matthew 5:21-43.

38. Matthew 7:22-23

39. Matthew 10:37-39

40. Matthew 16: 24-25

41. John 8:58

42. Exodus 3:14

43. John 14:6

44. You can watch the recording here: https://www.youtube.com/watch?v=QagzdvzzHBQ ot search for "What the World Needs Now - for Virtual Orchestra."

45. Matthew 5:43-45

46. Tom A. Jones and Steve D Brown, *The Kingdom of God, Volume 2: The Sermon and the Life* (Spring, Texas, Illumination Publishers, 2011), 166-167.

47. Jones and Brown, 178

48. Mark 4:10-11

49. John 8:7

50. Luke 7:36-50

51. Carolyn Custis James, *Malestrom: How Jesus Dismantles Patriarchy and Redefines Manhood* (Grand Rapids: Zondervan Reflected, 2022), 139.

52. Luke 19:1-10

53. John Ortberg, Twitter post, February 28, 2023, 8:30 p.m., https://twitter.com/johnortberg/status/1630742160931684358. (accessed February 28, 2023). At this writing, they are no longer called tweets, but postings on X.

54. Luke 6:45

55. Matthew 16:16-18

56. Matthew 18:17

57. John 13:34-35

58. Matthew 7:7-8

59. Greely, 169.

60. Greely, 93

61. Mark 9:1

62. Acts 4:20

63. Mary Oliver, "Have You Ever Tried to Enter the Long Black Branches, *West Wind* (New York; Houghton Mifflin, 1997).

64. Matthew 10:39

65. John 16:33

66. Matthew 5:3

67. John 15:11

68. Luke 24:52

69. Mary Oliver, "Don't Hesitate," *Swan* (Boston: Beacon Press). Reprinted by the permission of The Charlotte Sheedy Literary Agency as agent for the author. Copyright © 2010, 2017 by Mary Oliver with permission of Bill Reichblum.

70. Thomas Jones, God's Perfect Plan for Imperfect People (Spring, Texas: Illumination Publishers, 2020).

71. https://www.merriam-webster.com/dictionary/captivate.

72. Hebrews 12:1-2

73. John 21:15-25

74. Mary Oliver, "The Vast Ocean Begins Just Outside Our Church: The Eucharist," *Thirst* (Boston Beacon Press). Reprinted by the Permission of The Charlotte Sheedy Literary Agency as agent for the author. Copyright © 2006 by Mary Oliver with Permission of Bill Reichblum.

75. 2 Corinthians 4:8

76. Nouwen, p.17

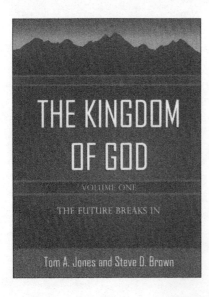

Books by
Tom A. Jones

www.ipibooks.com

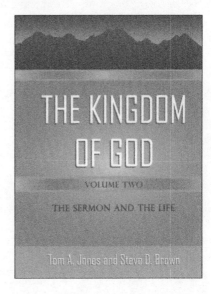

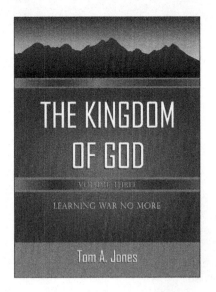

Books by
Tom A. Jones

www.ipibooks.com

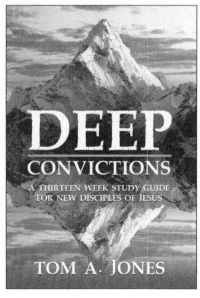

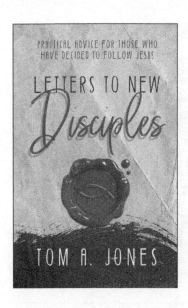

Books by
Tom A. Jones

www.ipibooks.com

Books by
Tom A. Jones

www.ipibooks.com

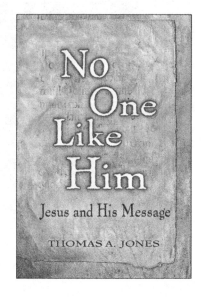

Welcome to the New

ILLUMINATION PUBLISHERS
www.ipibooks.com

www.ipibooks.com

Made in the USA
Monee, IL
19 August 2025